The A List

Launched to mark our forty-fifth anniversary, the A List is a series of handsome new editions of classic Anansi titles. Encompassing fiction, nonfiction, and poetry, this collection includes some of the finest books we've published. We feel that these are great reads, and the series is an excellent introduction to the world of Canadian literature. The redesigned A List books will feature new cover art by noted Canadian illustrators, and each edition begins with a new introduction by a notable writer. We can think of no better way to celebrate forty-five years of great publishing than by bringing these books back into the spotlight. We hope you'll agree.

ALSO BY LYNN CROSBIE

ANTHOLOGIES
Click
Plush
The Girl Wants To

FICTION
Life Is About Losing Everything
Dorothy L'Amour
Paul's Case

POETRY
Liar
Missing Children
Pearl
VillainElle
Miss Pamela's Mercy

Lynn Crosbie

Queen Rat

New and Selected Poems

This edition published in 2014 by
House of Anansi Press Inc.
110 Spadina Avenue, Suite 801
Toronto, ON, m5v 2k4
Tel. 416-363-4343
Fax 416-363-1017
www.houseofanansi.com

Distributed in Canada by
HarperCollins Canada Ltd.
1995 Markham Road
Scarborough, ON, m1b 5m8
Toll free tel. 1-800-387-0117

Distributed in the United States by
Publishers Group West
1700 Fourth Street
Berkeley, CA 94710
Toll free tel. 1-800-788-3123

House of Anansi Press is committed to protecting our natural environment. As part of our efforts, the interior of this book is printed on paper that contains 30% post-consumer recycled fibres, is acid-free, and is processed chlorine-free.

18 17 16 15 14   1 2 3 4 5

Library and Archives Canada Cataloguing in Publication

Crosbie, Lynn, 1963–, author
Queen rat / by Lynn Crosbie ; [introduction by Michael Turner].

Poems.
Issued in print and electronic formats.
ISBN 978-1-77089-832-5 (pbk.).—ISBN 978-1-77089-293-4 (html)

I. Title.

PS8555.R61166Q4 2014   C811'.54   C2014-902700-1
                                                 C2014-902701-X

Library of Congress Control Number: 2014938781

Cover design: Brian Morgan | Cover illustration: Michael Cho
Typesetting: ECW Type & Art, Oakville

We acknowledge for their financial support of our publishing program the Canada Council for the Arts, the Ontario Arts Council, and the Government of Canada through the Canada Book Fund.

Printed and bound in Canada

INTRODUCTION
by Michael Turner

LYNN CROSBIE'S *Queen Rat: New and Selected Poems* first appeared in 1998. Less a poet's book than a greatest hits instigated by its publisher, the collection nevertheless represents Crosbie's strongest work in the genre at that time. The book includes selections from her first three titles, *Miss Pamela's Mercy*, *VillianElle*, and *Pearl*, while new works "Fredo Pentangeli," "Presley," and "Alphabet City" hint at what readers might expect in the future from a writer interested in serial or concept-oriented bookworks. For Crosbie, that future arrived in 1997, with the publication of her collagist *Paul's Case*.

With the imminent re-issue of *Queen Rat*, another future is upon us. In "Composition as Explanation" (1925), Gertrude Stein writes, "Nothing changes from generation to generation except the thing seen and that makes a composition." In other words, times change, but the elements remain the same; we merely find different ways to organize and distribute them. Today, what is *seen* includes the Internet, the results of which are new compositional forms like the Facebook wall and the tweet. This is the kind of proposition I would offer up to Crosbie at one of the now-defunct bars she so brilliantly models in "Alphabet City" — had nothing changed and those bars not closed.

As a writer roughly the same age as Crosbie, someone I saw a lot of in the 1990s when I was reading in Toronto and she was reading in Vancouver, we have shared more than a few conversations together. Not only about writing, but about everything from metaphysics to the pants worn by the person serving us. Regardless of the content, these conversations would often get intense, where my *Why are we here, Lynn?* was met with her *Pffft!*, when there was something life-and-death about our server's ass.

The last time Crosbie and I spoke to each other was in the mid-2000s, when I showed up at her house unannounced and was greeted like Fredo by his brother Michael, in both "Fredo Pentangeli" and its referent, *The Godfather*. It was a greeting that recalled "I take flight, my mouth bruised," not from a kiss, as Michael kisses Fredo, but from the effort required to keep my mouth shut, from saying something I might regret later. (Of course I should have phoned first — what was I thinking?) From there I retreated to a bar, and then to my hotel room, where I wrote her a letter instead.

Looking through that letter now (unsent), I see that I recorded some of what I wanted to discuss with Crosbie when I called on her that day. For example, Crosbie is a confessional poet or, like the performance artist interested in *performativity*, she is interested in the confession as both a process and a form, the only apparatus "huge enough," as Sylvia Plath said of Ted Hughes upon first seeing him, to support her baroque lyric style. Her interest in confessional writing is present in her Ph.D. dissertation (on Anne Sexton). It is also present in her interest in portraiture, the fictive (Fredo) and the non-fictive (Pamela Des Barres) personae she inhabits, both of whose ambitions and injuries allow her to activate her own.

To riff on Crosbie, quoting Michael Ondaatje in "Alphabet City": *these are the known (By them)*. What is less known, or rather what is less spoken of with respect to Crosbie's practice, is a feminism that insists that if men and women are equal, then they are equal in their transgressions as well as in their virtues. Miss Pamela (Des Barres), the form and figure of her VillianElle, her Pearl, Paul's Karla Homolka, Dorothy (Stratten) L'Amour, the biographer of her *Liar* are all women who must be understood not as victims but as willing agents in their negotiations with rock stars, men's magazine publishers, murderous spouses, and mendacious ex-boyfriends.

Indeed, it is Crosbie's brand of feminism, stated or otherwise, that had award-winning *Toronto Star* journalist Rosie DiManno threatening to "rake my fingernails across her face" if she saw the *Paul's Case* author on the street. Or as Governor General's Award–winning poet Anne Szumigalski wrote in her review of *Queen Rat* for *Quill & Quire*, "A word of warning: Crosbie seems to be fascinated by violence" — an *avertissement* that implies the book is not a trenchant and poetic enquiry into violence and gender relations (à la Margaret Atwood's more restrained *Power Politics*) but the product of a passive voyeuristic fascination, where both its author and its reader are innocents at risk.

DiManno and Szumigalski are writers from another time; both have little patience for the high-low conflation that came to characterize Pop Art, conceptualism, and postmodernism. This too was something Crosbie and I had struggled with in the 1990s: what it meant to be the youngest of the old. But the years have moved us along, introduced new readers and writers to the culture, and the challenge to those born at the squiggly end of the baby boom is to speak as the oldest of the young, something to which Crosbie — the reclining Queen Rat on the cover of the first edition of this book — has risen.

To my grandmother Mary,
for Emma and the snakes,
for everything you've taught me,
with love.

Contents

Pearl

Fredo Pentangeli

i. Gabriel

My mother is lighting candles,
I am screaming. She smooths goose oil into
my chest as I purple with pneumonia.
Poor Fredo, they whisper,
and my father watches from the corner.
He covers his face.

                My father asks me to stop
at the market. He is selecting fruit, holding
it to his lips when the guns ignite.
Thrown back he staggers to the curb.
I am crawling toward him as the black car
retreats. He is bleeding; oranges tumble from
his coat. I sit on the curb and cover my face,
crying, Papa —

And the Angel departed from me.

ii. Raphael

Moe slapped me, a backhand. Your weakness,
he said; the cocktail girls scattered,
adjusting their aprons and stocking seams.
I have been drinking steadily, waiting for Michael.
The room is filled with streamers and whores.
Johnny Fontane sings Fly Me to the Moon
and cracks his knuckles, I see Tom first.
His gentle eyes frighten me, they are obsidian,
admonitory. Michael caresses
my face; before defending me,
he empties the room.

It is his low deadly voice that murmurs to me,
You are my brother and I love you, that sentences
Moe with a gesture:

His life strains away on a massage table, *chien andalou.*
Unlucky, is what Michael says.

iii. Lucifer

Why should your brother have all the power Fredo?
You can be a part of this: we know you are an intelligent
man.
               Johnny Ola's voice in my ear,
sibilant and true.
There will be sunshine and clear seas in Cuba.
Orange blossoms spill from his mouth.
The tropical palms sway, a chorus line, heavy with fruit.
He sleeps by the window, I tell him, I could open the drapes.
Just to frighten him.
Later, the guns sound in cannonade; Michael is pale with betrayal.
Someone close to us, he says, with certainty.

I think of husking coconuts, drinking their warm milk.
I see that I am ashamed.

iv. Mulciber

Michael takes me to the cabana;
I am hot and flustered.
The Havana sun beats on our striped umbrella,
I drink banana daiquiris and Michael sips
club sodas, cool and self-possessed.

Why don't we ever talk, I ask, flustered by his
attention, his quiet kindness.

I was so mad at you, I begin, and his patient smile
disarms me. My admission settles, the residue of pulp
and ice. Another! I call, rattling my glass. Please.

Mama said I wasn't hers, I tell Michael. That I was
left by the Gypsies. He holds my hand.

As he swoons in the nightclub he will seize
the railing, deciphering my plans.

The clock is easing to midnight: lovers embrace
and stardust falls.

Michael grabs me amid the pandemonium and kisses
me, hard, on the lips.

You broke my heart, he says.
I take flight, my mouth bruised,
for he is righteous, and he hath
taken arms against perfidy:
he, who is like God.

v. Michael

My mother is at rest. I kneel by her coffin
with my sister.

My long exile weighs on me.

I'm an orphan now, I beseech my brother.

Not stupid, like everyone says,
I'm smart and I want respect.
I told him, in faint imitation,
of the father, of the son who cast me out:

You're nothing to me.

And he draws me near, his eyes finding
judgement.

I accept his love and forgiveness,
lowering into the rowboat with his assassin
and his child: I tell him how I catch fish by
saying Hail Marys.

But Michael called for his son. And we two
rowed out alone. My lure catching the light,
my head canting in prayer —

Michael saw this from the window. He heard the
gunshots and bowed his head as I had not lived
but died in a state of grace.

Now and at the hour of our deaths, he prays:

I fall from his sight.

Presley

*Pet-crazy Dana Caneberry has kept her dead puppy Presley
on ice in her refrigerator freezer for the past two years, right
next to the frozen peas and TV dinners — because she just
can't stand to part with the pitiful pooch.*

— "Frozen Pup-Sicle," *Weekly World News*, April 1998

Priscilla arched her back and hissed when I brought
him home, her black fur rising like garter snakes.
Two little ones are double trouble,
but when I saw them kids take a knife to him,
my hands flew in the air like I was catching a moonstone.
He trembled against me, and I told him, All your trials soon be over.
Singing it some: his tail beating like a little white scarf,
caught in some king's fingers.

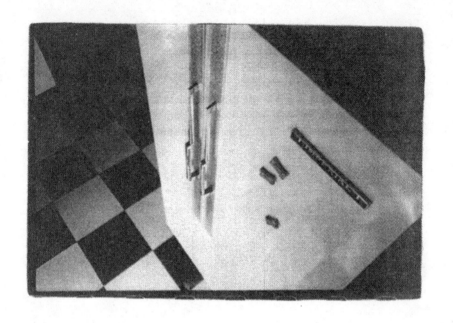

He can't hardly walk, my mother said. Would you
look at that. Presley was sleepy a little and making
his way over, harum scarum, bumping into chairs,
legs bent like tiny wishbones. He's just a yellow
cur, she said, as I kissed him flush on the mouth.
I told her, That's alright, that's alright now Mama:
in the sunlight his ears crown, golden.

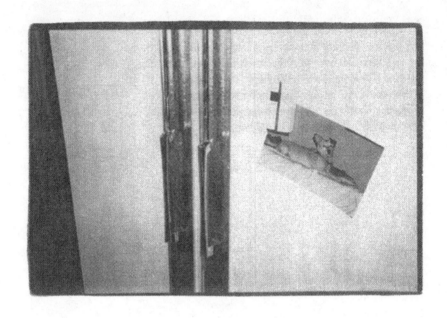

I never had a dog before: I've had a change of
habit. Brushing Presley and cutting his nails,
I watch his fur flying like dandelion seeds and ten
crescent moons on my new wall-to-wall.
Filling a basin with warm soapy water, I ease
him into the bath. When the fleas jump I snap them in my
fingers; he looks back as cool as can be.
His head in the darkening pool, its ivory nimbus.

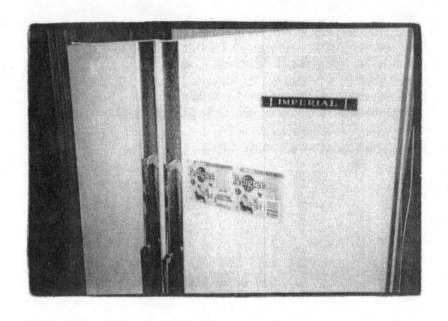

Had a man named Red in my life for some time,
a roustabout I hired to fix up my kitchen.
With long sideburns and a pompadour;
he cleaned his teeth with an ivory pick.
Jumped like catfish on a pole
when I touched him, said I had warm little hands.
He got some girl in trouble, left.
Thinking about him, I get lonely.
Presley brings over a slipper.
I remember how Red's hair smelled
when it was wet and slick with Prell.

Presley's pulling hard on his new leash;
I rush against the choke collar.
He sees a pile of leaves and jumps right in
like he's clam-digging. I take his lead
and roll around some, kicking up a tiny sunset.
I watch him chase a monarch:
he leaps and falls, keeps trying. My heart aches
as I imagine falling this way, deep into love
that takes wing, and leaves.

He sleeps in a kennel I made out of my closet,
usually starts crying after midnight to come see me.
I always end up bringing him to my bed
and he curls up on the pillow beside me while I read.
Tonight I am looking through travel brochures,
wondering at all the things I've never seen.
This here's the Memphis necropolis, I tell him.
And look at these pink gardenias floating out to sea
from the Kahoolawe shore. I start to feel sad,
knowing I'll never go anywhere, wanting
to race through Maui driving a pink Jeep,
with my dog beside me, his flowered bandana
whipping the wind. He noses my face, settles
in the crook of my arm. *O, lovely you,*
I croon, reaching for my ukulele.
The plucked strings sound like stars chiming;
I see the sky crest like a Big Kahuna.
The light of the moon pours in blue, tenders me
this magic night of nights with you.

The nights are getting longer. Presley and I
have taken to eating outside and cooling off
under the weeping willows. He's still a tiny thing,
looks like a plush toy upended in the grass.
Cassandra peers over the fence after hanging
her laundry, and makes small talk as she coaxes Priscilla
over her shoulder; her long white dress ruffles
in the first sweet breeze.
Her face begins to glow and I hear Presley whining:
he's staring up at something I can't see,
working his legs like pistons.
What's the matter darling?
I am rushing over to him and Cassandra says,
He knows his time has come. The whole sky
is suddenly barren and black and I am afraid.
The crickets and cicadas are whirring;
Presley's baleful eyes seek mine. Singed in ginger are
two irises, mandarin, vermilion, flaming stars.

I left the door open for a minute and he ran away.
Priscilla leaped to the window and switched her tail,
her eyes gleaming like cut emeralds.
I walked up and down the streets, calling for him.
At dawn I crumpled on the porch with his
biscuits and Puppy Chow, my voice ragged and weak.
Come on home — I kept on until I was whispering,
my blood running every time I saw a flash of white:
Cassandra's skirt, scrolling along the curb; a kite
caught in the trellis; paper alight on the wind.
I fell asleep for a while and heard a voice
as hard as thunder, making a melody, he's gone gone gone —
The rain fell on my face and I woke up shaking.
I dreamed of King Creole, slipping from my fingers
and swimming away, his scales glittering like heraldry.

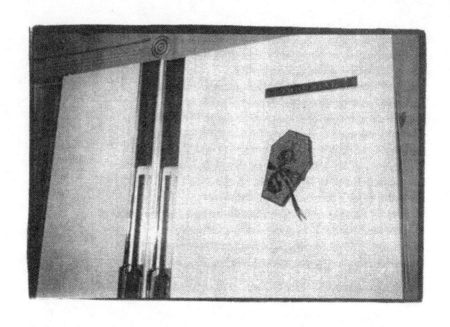

I have arranged his things around me in a circle:
his collar and hedgehog squeak-toy, the little blue sweater
he wore on cool night walks. I am praying hard and shaking
like a leaf on a tree. Oh Lord, my God,
if you could return him to me I'll never let
him go, if you could just —
I fall over running to the door and there's a tall stranger
looking scared and wary. I had a spinout,
he says. Wrecked my Harley, I never even seen him.
What are you telling me for, I start, as he holds his arms out.
He is holding Presley and I reach for him,
wondering why he's so still. I stroke his matted fur,
soundlessly, until it blurs, a pale rose.
He's not dead, I say, he's sleeping. His body is rigid
and broken; my hands are pressing him straight.
The stranger nods and says, I'm sorry.
I'm so sorry, he says, as I fall to my knees,
Come back —

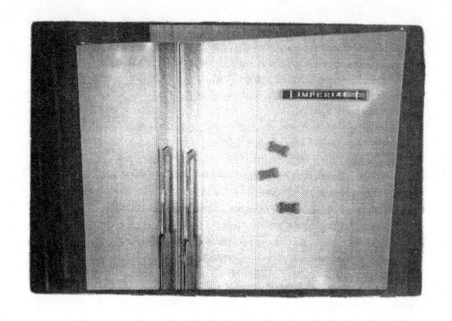

Waking up forgetting to remember he's not there,
my pillow next to me, cold and smooth. I can't feel
this bad, I can't —
I cleaned the kitchen all night long, bleached the floor,
defrosted the Imperial, and began placing white roses
on the shelves. I carried Presley over and rested him
among the flowers; carefully closed him inside
and replaced the plug. After a while the ice sparkled in his hair,
riming the roses, his lashes and brow.
When I walk the floor nights, grief like a stone in my throat,
I find myself opening the door and petting him,
telling him that it makes no difference where I go or what I do.
The frost blows into my face like the breath of an angel:
I feel my life slowing down, becoming still. Immutable,
my love lies like a pretty ghost, glorious and milky-blue.
And you know I'll always be loving you, I say,
spelling it into the small snow the whole night through.

Note
Photographs by Bruce McDonald

Alphabet City

Allan Gardens, 1994

He was a difficult person to get to know. For one thing he was obsessed with coincidences.

— Daniel Jones, "The Birth of a Minor Canadian Poet"

I left my little black jacket at Diane's and he forgot his raincoat. Susan drove us downtown, telling us about the tantric orgasm; he offered to pick up our coats. He called me to meet him, and we went to Hernando's Hideaway. We talked about Daniel's death, and I asked if he was depressed. I hardly ever talk about killing myself anymore, he said.

He disliked Daniel's fiction and I disagreed. He told me a photograph of the two of them together had fallen from a book the week before he died, which troubled him. At the S/M store I tried on a vinyl skirt and he told the salesperson he was my father.

We walked to Allan Gardens, and disagreed some more. Daniel's writing is economical and pure, I said. I thought he gave up after writing poetry, he said. He said some other things, and I didn't see him again. I did not tell him that the last time I saw Daniel he told me he had spoken in his sleep. He said: I hate lyrical poetry:

> *Though Amaryllis dance in green*
> *Like fairy queen;*
> *And sing full clear* (Anonymous, 16th century)

The spring that silvers your bones cools beneath the panes of glass,
    in the field of green
where I have come with your friend who creeps beside me,
    pale with loss. Serene,
I imagine he is you, where cosmology reveals a pool of goldfish
    as inverse suns.
There is a frail banana tree, a border of white amaryllis fastens stars

33

to the carapace of moss, the emerald lily pads are diadems
    that coronate each one.
He lowers himself to sing full clear, your faults, the rows of cactus
    sliced with scars.
And with jaded pleasure, compels me to see the earth devour you;
    to look on in ill unease,
as ashen petals fall beneath the gold, like the ruined fruit of banana trees.

(For DM: aabcbcdd)

Black Bull

Elvis is Alive

— *National Examiner,* August 1986

This will be the last summer we spend outside here. The one great patio bar with pool tables, a severed bull's head, and room upstairs, where

William and Marjorie once sold books and scraps of paper for dope, cooking one potato each day, the sun blocked out with lace curtains.

I first met Steve Goof and wore all of his rings, dragon's skull and silver urchins, while he chalked his cue and swept off his coat. Black, lined in lurid red: matador.

A skinhead (SKINS tattooed to his forehead) followed me out onto the street, still carrying his pitcher, offering me a handkerchief covered in someone else's blood: *because your eyes are so sad.*

We invited Lisa's mother who smoked Sweet Caporals, drank straight gin.

Greg held my ankles in *the high Roman fashion.* My legs, in Egyptian tights, on his lap; he traced the sphere of the ankh, his dog panting beside us. You're a good girl, he said, and I saw the hieroglyph on her head: a diamond.

There was a cloudburst, and we stayed out in the rain without umbrellas,
talking about love. Janet brushing away her black forelock, explaining
Ecstasy — you are so beautiful, you want to kiss yourself,

the summer drenching our bare legs stretching on and on my birthday
we have met to celebrate. Our impending trip to Memphis, four girls
in tight tiger dresses and backcombed hair. There is some breeze; our
eyes are outlined like cats', like the catfight we will have in Kentucky,
3 Leos and one Scorpio in tears,

Carol curled up on the backseat, Elvis used to yell **I walk catlike,**

at the grave we are kittenish, as if someone has died.

Cameron House

THIS IS PARADISE
— Cameron House painting, circa 1985

These Are the Killed

(By them)

Handsome Ned smiles easily in Stetson, silver-tipped collar and
boots, slips smack into the darkness and

George, a scientist who studied random patterns — duck feet
on snow — who liked to do the chicken, legs flailing, arms in
semaphore, drops dead this way;

Brat X hanging from the rafters: **I know my life is getting harder;**

Richard who played chess, cracking his knuckles to release *natural
endorphins,* his body undiscovered for days, the smell

35

of purple sage, riders slit their wrists, drink to death.

Carl, the last of these Mohicans, calls from his quiet corner: **right on,**
later all the punks would steal this phrase, after the dust settled

around the campsite, Bob would crawl into his tent with his Sylum
clippings and asphyxiate himself; at a haunted house one summer, I
screamed as the lights went out and fell to the floor:

what's wrong with you, he asked, as he led me back into the light,

toward the yellow birds, slowly turning in the shooting gallery.

These Are the Killed

(By me)

A murder of crows; witches,
Nicholas, Jerry, early friends of mine
Katie with the heel of a shoe (in self-defence)
and Penny: a necklace of bloodstones,
fire-lasso.

> Michael Ondaatje signs **Billy the Kid** in 1993:
> *For Lynn wlnonolwirs, ni*

D anforth

Immensity is within ourselves.

— Bachelard

I now seek a phenomenological determination of images:

calamari, the contours of the octopus head, its tentacles push the
currents like the images that provoke dreams

of rounded flesh, undulating limbs that caress and asphyxiate, the
membranous skin is dotted a Morse code —

eight trips to the Danforth for black olives, feta cheese, the Virgin
Mary in a circle of red and gold,

to visit the Moon Cave:

(1987)

The small back room is dark and blue; plaster stalactites hang from
the ceiling, there is the sound of bats. The Moon Cave cocktail is
aquamarine, the accordion player performs national anthems of the
world. Comes over and offers to *play something gypsy.* A serenade.

The caves of the moon that curve beyond the pale lakes, a rustle of wings

the taste of sapphires, the sense of an *immensity within you,*

the earth that dreams the moon, each night

suspended from the limestone lip, the liminal sky.

Elvis Monday (1983–) Haiku

It's like an old song / everything seems to be / just like an old song to me
— Groovy Religion

Beverley Tavern,
The Silver Dollar Room, The
Apocalypse, The

Slither or Soup Club,
The Drake, The Edgewater and
The El Mocambo

Echo Papa

Unnamed

Janet's black eye a
yellow starfish: *I'm going
to be great tonight*

Steve sings *Suzanne* in
the style of Elvis while Marj
cooks hamburgers, live.

Mr. Gregory

Orange Reality

from Mississauga:
*you got the devil in you
woman,* he frets and

Someone suggests they
practise. Jam for five minutes:
We're sounding too tight.

shakes his yellow hair.
An old high-school friend, dropout —
Look, *the devil's gone*

I'm getting to it.
Crowd hectors, one bass line starts —
G G G A C

Groovy Religion

The Ether Brothers

*you take the car, I'll
take drugs.* Valium Funk starts,
William falls; his dance

Because they do this
For each performance: a vial
of ether, tuneless

F ort Goof (1985–91)

They told me he was bad, but I knew he was sad,
I'll never forget him — the leader of the pack

— The Shangri-las

I had met him before, opening a car with a coat hanger, other times. He
and his big dog, Dirt, all of them roaming the streets on skateboards,
bicycles, in armour (chain-belts, big black boots). That he slept in a cage,
in a space fortressed by electrical wire, gangplank entrance off Baldwin
Street. Skittering across this in high heels, night after night, half in love.

Coming over after-hours, standing on the slag-roof by the hills of
wheels spokes metal cans one derelict Mercedes, two stars visible,
he spills peach schnapps into my mouth from his, bliss.

Wet muzzles of dogs on my ankles, random killings. Trying to keep a
low profile for almost seven years. Coaxing him to read his lyrics for
us, my head on the dog's belly, a long flowered dress:

started out as recreational / now it's getting quite habitual —

to draw him like a hermit crab outside of himself. Kick this. Be a man
for once in your life and see me to the door. Kick that, higher.

With inappropriate presents of lavender bath salts and white roses,

chocolate hearts in foil; the night he has planned to have me (and five
scared friends) thrashed for violating the code. I'm heat score, he says
and I smile. His friends paw the floors, anxious.

Later he falls to his knees *I'm sorry I'm sorry,* drunk he would

save my life, several times, film me in handcuffs, Cisco coming up the
stairs looking for some action in **Goofs Take 29**; I am merely holding

the cuffs and am therefore not compromising myself, I say. It is 6 A.M. and time to weave out through the alleys

in my gown I am quite soignée, and I have a little lie down in an alley before two kind policemen pick me up and drive me home. I imagine that there were rats, lying like tiny babies, in my arms,

like dolls: pills and drinking less and less food: **alcoholiday turned alcoholocaust,** the song that he read when I lay in that gutter (looking at the stars &c.)

Besieged by skinheads *(we are 138 strong and will kill you),* I see a little crown when I pass by where it ended and began. With sledgehammers and chainsaws, his eyes looking ahead, somewhere clear,

a clean table, plexiglass shower, plants in casement window. I am invited to Dirt's wake this May. With more flowers, a round of toasts to the dog that died in Mexico, lolling in the sun and startled by all the water, the purity.

Clean white bed he slips neatly into each night, hair still shaved in the one thin line

I crossed to meet him, like a pirate wild for the black flag,

that signals danger, night riders, the other marauder

who turns around and smiles at you, over shark fins, water as black as your treacherous heart.

Gladstone Hotel (1985)

The whole rhythm section was the purple gang . . .

It was a blizzard out there, but King Elvis (Toronto's first impersonator + Subway Elvis) was performing at the great hotel where Sweet Daddy

Siki's purple Cadillac surfs by,

and there is mud wrestling, some country and western in the Bronco Room.

He is wearing a gold lamé jacket with unfinished edges, black slacks.
Looks nothing like Elvis but we dance on the chairs as he sings. Those
lush segue ways I said I don't wanna I don't wanna be don't wanna be tied,

that old hook — sm. hip-swivelling, a tired blonde girlfriend clicking
her nails to the beat, smashed, we ask him to sing **Smoke on the Water,**
Elvis-style,

and he gives it a shot which is why he's the King:

Frank Zappa and his buddies were at the best place in town, some
crewcut with a flare-gun burned the place to the ground, yes!

There is a little car accident later and I tip the driver generously, record
snowfalls, ice, and fast winds. I appreciate a little showmanship.

Huron Street (1986–90)

Kites fly up
Kites fly down
They touch the ground
Pretty kite
Nice and bright
Such a nice sight

— first poem (age 6)

The Epitome apartments lay south of College; Coach House Press north,
through a walkway and courtyard, flights of rickety stairs. I am writing
poems and feel it is a sign, living here,

slanted ceilings, mice, a view of the alley. Where Jesse stands in a toga, setting fire to garbage and the nervous old transvestite (his door marked *skirt, my pretty name)* wrings his hands. Criminals, thieves; Mike the con who gives me a lift in his Camaro one day, crushed in between three pretty girls with shag haircuts and skintight jeans.

I am writing while Steve becomes more absorbed in his *projects:* lining up superhero figures in action poses, underlining entries in the *TV Guide* (we have no television), writing lyrics he will not perform for eight years

with Translove Airways. One is about me, how mean I've become, popping out Plastic-Man's head so it topples the whole row like tenpins. *Why'd you want to be that way?*

We broke everything before he left, windows plates glasses, and later I would remember him. Standing wanly by the window in old pyjama bottoms, scissors and highlighters, broken

unloved. I wrote about the chicken-baby doll he gave me, and he read it years later and we were sad about the ups and downs of it all.

I remember going through the walkway after signing my first book contract with Coach House,

sure that everything was waiting to be found (his Hello Kitty notes that still pop from books and boxes),

that the world was coming true.

> *[now that you seem so much closer than you've ever been]*

> Translove Airways: "I Think the World Is Coming True"

42

Isabella (+ Yonge) 1982

Going with the flow it's all the same to me
— Motörhead

I have dreaded this, moving to Toronto. On the VIA train, leaving
Montreal, I think of the '67 Exposition. The rows of pavilions, the
athletes' honeycombed quarters, the geodesic dome that flowered
and burned. Remembering the city this way,

lost in the Mont Royal cemetery, looking for my grandmother's
grave and never finding it. From the woods the plots are like anthills.

Abbreviated angels are raising their wings.

I am frightened by a man in the bar-car who threatens to throw me
from the train. Threading back to my seat I meet Claire and ask her
to pretend she knows me. The man in hot pursuit.

Leaves when he sees my head on her shoulder. My first friend,

a fashion illustrator and heavy-metal queen. She shows me around,
we visit the Gasworks and she shakes her long hair, listening to the
cover band: *That's the way I like it baby*

(I don't want to live forever).

I am a punk with two inches of spiked hair, a fish out of water.
Trying to breathe. Sending long letters home and cultivating a
depression that borders on nerve,

I will cut my legs with knives and slice my fingers with broken
glass. And call up Claire.

We examine snakes in the Exotic Pet Store, and shop for eyelet and lace, she loans me her apartment and I persist. Hooking up, deeper into the city, until there is someone else,

and someone else.

I see her again, for the last time. We eat lunch at The Tender Trap where Sinatra sings about this and that:

I've been up and down and over and out and I know one thing.

Picking myself up from this strange corner and cutting out. My first friendship like a shiver, the silken legs of the tarantula, that navigates from wrist to elbow, feeling its way around.

James Joyce Pub (1996)

a girl loveable in the extreme.

— Ulysses

and we met there at eight or so Elizabeths never on time and her body blooms in black with slits some smooth white showing and her dark lips curl you think of the edges of mussels we drowned in lime in the cabbageleaf green of this place she says the shamrocks catch in her throat with the harp goes the tenor O Sweetheart

we find an abandoned grocery cart and push Michael fast and let go O tragic dyinglooking his ankle twisted not letting him go but her eyes meeting mine like 2 big poppies shadows I suppose of nights

you wear a clean shift and powder and there is some story her beautys unfolding like petals and rotten things like swallowing a ring she gave back of course and cleaned like opium whites your bones though you are sick and your hair a bit loose from tumbling

through nights with her theyre lovely something goes through me all

like needles she carves her hand with a knife before she leaves and I
am thinking of her on the sea her catoninetails Im certain in a carpetbag

Ive cut myself and she presses her hand to mine our blood flowers
tulips are we sisters then will you remember her away in red sand sun
kisses her shoulders and moonlight blue her legs in the salt water lime
sea and yes I said yes I will Yes.

Kensington Market (Summer 1987)

The Market this night is deserted, after three, feral cats
    comb for fishheads; diablerie
mists rising from sewer gratings, the moon through scaffolding,
    crescented.

There is the sound of breaking glass, Carol and I see clothes
    drift from a window, inspirited —
ghosts; a junkie is tossing his girlfriend's dresses, black, edged
    in jessamine and picotee.

He knocks her down and hammers her face, her hair in his hands,
    his fingers signeted
with spiked rings; she twists and cries. When we call out,
    he pivots with cruel celerity,

Leave her alone — slowly we approach him, he says
    Yr in the wrong neighbourhood pussy.
And advances, mouth arched in hatred, tendon-cut arms taut,
    sick with dread

I stare him down; we gather her things, barrettes and beads, a little purse,
    chenille bedspread,
and look at her: the girl's face is diamonded with bruises,
    green and purple nebulae.

She shakes, her thin body an atlas, the street's colours, shapes, in relief,
    and faceted.
Points of light shine from her elbows, ankles, her back reveals
    sharp vertebrae,

like cat's teeth, tearing rotting flesh, to subsist; she turns to him,
    slight honeybee,
to recover the sweetness, the sting; droning that they are overfed

with opiates she knows are tender, hard, familiar with this alchemy,
    she holds his sleeve
and kisses him; Carol and I turn, empty our hands; our shadows follow,
    disquieted.

L ansdowne and Bloor (1984–86)

> *altered consciousness*
> *NOT* altered consciousness
>
> — bp Nichol, *The Martyrology,* Book Six

sick in bed speed & percodan lisa & i share a plate of rice
leave some for the cats their tails rise like stirring snakes, furious.

our hair bleached white i own two party dresses
study statistics each night while andrew plays hot chocolate,
arithmetical problems: *heavens in the backseat of my Cadillac
let me take you there,* steve working as a sailor drunk one night
on waterbed yells **man overboard.**

watch the sunrise, bowls of peas & chocolate, walking through the
underpass by the junkyards, i take off my heels & run, reckless

with love for someone else, who wears pink socks & sleeps with a
machete, who beats someone up the morning we meet, beats him

blood rains down his face; he had stared at me & wouldn't leave.

share sm hash by the war memorial (verdigris angel & bayonet)
at queen & university, i describe this also how we slept like mice
his hand grazing my hip, his lips on my shoulder.

> a diary that is read & i am undone, there are
> two men, then none: producible numbers.

when i have left & am living in a cathouse on admiral road (pimp runs
in to clean his face where margaret has scratched him &c)

i think of lansdowne, moving in gunshots that night, the stripclub i
liked, where a girl left her fur coat with her sister & peeled off her
spangled bikini

old men gathered around, throwing pennies at her feet, i imagine
i have left this way

> a few articles to toss together

& spin, the rattle of loose change like maracas, when carnival begins.

Ministry of Love (1982–89)

Didn't time sound sweet yesterday? In a world filled with friends,
you lose your way.

— Scott Walker

Also known as the Church of the Fallen Elvis (and for after-hours,
Make My Bed in Hell torn as beer tickets) because they would only
ingest drugs and food of the baroque Elvis: cheeseburgers, Quaaludes,
Demerol, Fiorinal.

Where I met my closest friends still, and some of the filthiest people

47

alive: seducing girls through sedation, exposing themselves in front of moonlit windows, sleeping in amber clouds of vomit, taping hapless visitors:

i love you guys ill blow you i will if thats what it takes ill blow you.

Walls kicked into craters, Jerry holding court talking shit, coercing an ill woman to the back room who calls out, *I don't want to suck your cock,* what passes for a good story, what passes —

In the bathroom someone has written Hope for Me I Hope for You.

Parkdale warehouse hidden behind Queen and Bellwoods with stage-set lofts, where I sleep most of the time during rehearsals wake up angry and throw chairs, murmurs all night

from the kitchen, guys cranking cough syrup and Valium. My goldfish swims in dense limewater by the gaslight, prowling for oxygen

light. There are no windows, and soon we all desert the place. Where cockroaches cakewalk on the walls and all the spoons are black.

I came here to meet someone; we were together for five fitful years. He followed me home because he was locked out and didn't want to get his pale slacks dirty in the park.

He said things like that, *pale slacks.* Mesmerized (a lizard held in a palm, its flesh stroked in determined circles), I listened to him talk. About car accidents The Shaggs his father the nightclerk Jean Genet that love was a great big thing

beginning with one word. He left a note for me the day we met. On a square of green paper:

Niagara Falls (1994)

In the end, / The water was too cold for us.

— Robert Lowell

In August we head out four or five of us with overnight bags
bathing suit daywear a good evening gown bottles of gin and vodka
Names we call ourselves Marilyn Taffy Venus Penny Dreadful Sparklett

And visit the Main Drag the Wax Museum the House of Criminals
(we take turns in the electric chair lights flickering a charge)
Houses of Horror and Illusion

The moaning and shrieks it is pure black and we fall into
the light stopping for souvenir snowshakers viewfinders postcards
to see the Odditorium genie who lives in a bottle and squeaks hello

the Falls a glittering backdrop when we dance on the tables
of the rooftop bar singing and baiting each other the whole neon strip
lit up with signs heart-shaped waterbeds + jacuzzi the Oasis

Motel where we stay up late our legs bruised in T-shirts and Marilyn
in black panties cutting limes with an emery board Taffy reclining the
lioness imperial highness Venus in leather shorts with a bunch of bananas

posing legs split and pushup bras while Penny snaps pictures it's late and
the next morning we are dour in sunglasses pink camellias in our mouths
shoving our way to the front of the line we stand in yellow raincoats

at the prow of the Maid of the Mist   We huddle together our hair soaked
and tangled after entering the water's breakpoint as the spray lifted
and crashed we stepped back afraid of the water it was cold and ruthless

For years we would look at our pictures laughing at how drunk
how reckless we were   Laughing at Led Zeppelin until the waiter cried

Sparklett thrown out of the 7 Eleven for screaming nonononono — yes

She and I singing to the cab driver a song about diapers and big white pins
how the flowers looked our lips were flowers   Pictures I have since
discarded surprised at my own illusions

Hand in hand in pink and yellow a calyx   Saturated
suffering its weight and falling apart blossoms floating downstream
maids in the mist

Ossington and Bloor (1995)

Can you dig it.

— Jim Morrison, "The Opening of the Trunk"

I am waiting for Sara w/Michael
it is her birthday the sun is a groove lights
his jesus hair

yeah — I dig his eyes attack'd by
farout green & black. His purple-lips & vest,
a trip: mirrors velvet disrepair,

I hand her some potions love & power, mixed w/incense
& we go off to see the petstore, like,
time does not exist, just this cat (so fair).

Sara says, man, you two looked so happy,
going off to see the crickets,

(they are fed to other creatures) we touched their
bowed legs, salt-green, folded in prayer.

Petsitting (Kendal Avenue, 1988)

I just can't fit
I believe it's time for us to quit

I am petsitting two cats and a goldfish
hot August
     hardwood floors 7 rooms a palace

pyjama parties, Chris and I share some coke
I watch **The Bad Seed**
     scared all night little girls are scaling the walls,

he and Carol come back and I sleep in a bunk bed.

Steve visits twice, and knows that it is over.
Tony in residence,
     have to hide all the scotch,

but we read all day and hot nights pass, dressed in nurses' uniforms
with Marjorie, William,

we have a double date or two, deal hands of bad influence, misconduct:

three-cornered hats, couch cushions scattered.

We will spend seven years together. It all begins on this couch,
my hair wet, worried, he pats it dry. Tells me everything will be alright,
leaves a poem by my toes when I sleep.

Something about the way I sound, when I wake up

I call for him,

every day.

Queen Street West (1150) 1992

This coincidence of opposites (cold, methodical cruelty and boundless love)...

— Slavoj Žižek

Daniel and I have agreed to launch our books together: **Obsessions** and **Miss Pamela's Mercy.** He wants a hardcore band to play and has a formidable mailing list (I am soon embarrassed to overhear Jim Smith saying "who keeps putting me on fucking lists?").

We design an invitation. Pink. I decide there should be a cockroach on it, and Daniel meticulously clips one from an encyclopedia. William loans us the Drake, and Marjorie (my cover girl) acts as emcee and decorator, covering the walls with streamers and album covers:

Martin Denny's Tropical Sea Sounds; Claudine Longet; Tiny Bubbles.

Daniel calls and asks if I have a bullwhip he can borrow. When I arrive, dressed as Morticia, he is nervously arranging a pyramid of books. Dave Howard launches our books from a slingshot; we listen to Grasshopper, and read after Marj's flustered introductions.

She is wearing a spangled bridesmaid dress. Her voice squeaks: *I . . . don't know Daniel Jones very well . . .*

He comes out and whips the floor while a tape loop plays, his voice reciting his obsessions:

fuck it fit it kick kick it kick it.

Downcast, he signs my book with a drawing of a little cat while I sit around like the stuck-up belle of the ball.

A few weeks later, he tells my friend Nancy he was unhappy with the event. His face

squinting on the back cover, nightmarish faucet drip on the front that drove me crazy, fix that!

He called me his "partner in crimes." I think of us, happy, with our bugs and glue, imagining a kind of punk marriage, of him falling

from grace. At his own wedding he wore blue: what is essentially *flawed* in the reproduction of natural forms is the idea that there is *balance, harmony* in our own natures.

Water falling like torture, water that is not staunched, but simulated:

> *The blade of the knife. Pieces of blue. Slashing and slashing —*
> *There are no more words.*

Roncesvalles (Summer 1987)

see how they Fall   each frothing crest by

> *Christ a palm*   A Finger
> > *pointing into,*

— Steven Heighton

There are no September vacancies. Lisa and I have started walking the streets looking for somewhere to live; she walks slowly, stops

to pick up stones eggshell a leaf. Her odd step a swivel, slip
(as a child she sits under a silver tree, tinsel starlets her body cast),
we walk south on Roncesvalles, toward Lake Ontario. She misses the Pacific, remembers sailing paper ships rigged with tiny parasols, into Japan, how they

tumbled, spilling over rocks. The wavelets we make in the pools of water
on the sidewalks, our faces catching rain as if we are in tears, we walk

past the park, the summer has been hard. Carrying our cats on buses —
hers hangs from the window, screaming — looking for signs,
we see the pope statue and cross west,

we have broken glass against fountains at night, spells against love,
and we stand at this monument together and touch his white feet,
fingers laced across cold wet marble.

Like glass, sealed together with breath, our breath held to be blessed, something

we never forget. His holiness more tangible than the determination
that brought us further, to the edge of the water,

our toes drifting out, pale staysails, testing the tide.

Scream in High Park (July 19, 1993)

As it hath beene sundry times publickely acted, by the Right honourable . . .
— *(Midsummer Night's Dream)* Stationers' Register, October 8, 1600

10.05 *Enter Sky Gilbert, Master of the Revels*

I can hear snatches of Sky's work *Wake me, beauty, For I am asleep* from
behind the fence where I am waiting with bill bissett. The audience gives
him their hands, I see Hippolyta's crown shining as it is thrown to his feet,
rubies and sapphires tumbling, when I look up

                        (I will visit Sky one summer to watch
Dead Poets' Society *coq au vin* and endive salad, zebra pillows, shifting
uncomfortably in the heat

                    emanating from the beautiful boys.

Disoriented as the movie ends and the prettiest one, who plays Puck, has blown his brains out, we go our separate ways.

                    Some thoughts of *Captain, my Captain,*
how movies bury what is unequivocal — Sky and I falling apart, when the moon rises and the lights retreat.)

10.20 *Enter Helena*

I am holding bissett's T-shirt
                              [given to me with sections of an orange
for nerves]

wearing a white dress   [that looks like a tablecloth]

earrings that are little naked men.

Later, I will try to remember watching Michael though *I cannot truly say how we came here.* Summer wind lifts my hairpiece like cardinals' wings through the papers as though I am not afraid I [start up]

And I have found him like a jewel
Mine own, and not mine own.

10.30 *Enter David Donnell, as Peter Quince, a carpenter, representing Prologue*

Wasn't Lynn great? I can't get over it,

Donnell as talk-show host works his sleeves
his cue is past
                    and he is filled with *wanton energy.*

It will take years before I read his work and see
objects of beauty lit like lemons wet
quivering

below luminous stars and music trembling, to feel
a love supreme.

[Yes, it doth shine that night]

10.50 *Enter bill bissett, Duke of Athens [lords and attendants]*

th companeez n xcellent spirits
dreems uv aneething or
sew i feel

on *th green n bountiful hill side*
bissett nevr faltrs —
showers us   [attended by peaseblossom cobweb moth and
mustardseed]
                         with sorceree.

Sweet friends, to bed, is his summons, sew

veree lovlee.

T all Bars (1986–)

The Park Plaza Rooftop

If you are a writer press 18 and exit, left right
a plush ghost-Algonquin, ferns
framed drawings of its clientele.

Draw a handlebar moustache on Atwood,
a goatee. Call it LHOOQ:
decide *she has a hot ass.*

Sparkles (Top of the CN Tower)

Remember you will throw up on the way down.
Pose for a Polaroid, sidle out to the lookout point,

smoke a joint rolled in Tigerskins paper,
watch two lonely women dance *un slow,*
shuffling a little,

their skirts cut in A-lines, their lips moving:
the orchestra's yawning, they're sleepy I know.

Trader Vics *(High Above the Sparkling City)*

Order the most offensive drink on the menu
that will arrive on fire

decorated with umbrellas, a yellow bird, a Polynesian man
wearing a lei.

Overhear two businessmen chat up a woman who describes her
stretch marks to them: vivid

the purple flame on the lip of your bowl. Ask the bartender
if you can keep the skull-mug. When he declines, slip it in your jacket
and run like hell.

The Aquarius Lounge

Visit the 50th floor of the Manulife Building many times. Swoon
over the view of the city, all honeycombs and garnet.

Listen to the piano man sing Billy Joel songs, encourage him.

Write "Hi Sailor" on a napkin and pass it to a flustered customer.

Insist on Brandy Alexanders, sing Brandy yr a Fine Girl
while your brother shows his ass to the camera.

Look away when the waiter warns, ominously:

Do not do that again, sir . . . Take down your pants.

U nion Station (1983–84)

My hand draws back. I often sigh still
for the dark downward and vegetating kingdom
— Robert Lowell, "For the Union Dead"

Green and white boxcar heading west past
moulting ferris wheel pasture rows of houses each alike:

in los alamos this summer I see white tombstones
stuck fast in the hills. Desert flowers tumble

weeds brush the wheels and I am sometimes
sedated as the melon-pink of mountains rise sheets of

distant lightning shear the dark downward, of motion.
Moving back east past clarkson portcredit mimico

to union, half the regiment dead to me now I was
looking past the scorched fields toward a city

(a blessèd break)

from an angry family, jobs that are sweeter since:
cleaning houses on amphetamines, waitress in a diner

i got an eye in my beer, look up at empty socket and
tables trembling, spider delirium, the hoodlums in the back

who offer me rides home in the rain, a triumph, skidding off-centre,
what I have left behind in another city *(Ah spent the morning*
installin the pussy pad — let's roll)

over valleys and dirt paths, this city looms unknown
until I have turned over each rock and want to keep moving,

sliding into more desolate terrain. I often sigh still, their names faint
an abstract cemetery where I go with crepe myrtle (texas rose)

to offer myself, made of spirits,

       the conductor calls:

paterson Johnson tynkaluk adlai hazen cuddy dent trudi nixon lauzon
frechette ross burnham brand walcott sanders mcclintock dewdney
flahiff earl milchem wasson warlock kathy t payne

stops I miss, static, sleep,

train I ride half-dead

objects falling back, smaller, in perfect miniature: the line
of little cats' teeth, bridging sharp incisors, that comb the body,
drawing out tangles in long tined tracks.

Vive Karaoke (Kensington and Baldwin, 1993)

Tên Bán Nhac: "You Light Up My Life"

So many days: spent at the old Quoc Té. Formerly Peter's punks-drugs-
music clubhouse, now a karaoke bar — rumours of back alley garrotting,
gunshots. One night a Vietnamese gang gets close, is deflected by our
bracelets: sandalwood beads & glass Buddha. They sing for us instead
Now mothers tell your children, not to do what I have done.

I'd sit by my window, waiting for someone to sing me his song:
Afternoons are for Marjorie, we are alone in orange hooker wigs,
letting discs ride, clapping for each other. Our loneliness and pale
desires — her voice too much like air, and my one gig at the Paddock,
singing "I Fall to Pieces," falling to pieces I am so afraid.

[later at the bar by the Grand Ole Opry I
will sing the hell out of this song where Hank Williams rests, drinking
and writing, knowing that he is pulling up dead]

Nights with Chris or Richard or Andrew (dressed as John Shaft), other
serenades:

im just a jealous guy.

So many dreams, kept deep inside me: of blue smoke, the brilliant facets
of the mirrored ball, cocktails coursing through me, ice and tonic: wanting
to kiss everyone, to kill them (in one prism my green sleeves a praying
mantis). They ride Spadina north home, waving white

handkerchiefs I keep folded in my pocket
                                        made up, my tears are black.

Alone in my heart, but now you've come along: He isn't drinking anymore
but he follows me down Kensington, slipping away. Pretending I need
protection and I ask him to duck downstairs for a quick song. Dangerous,
what William calls **scaraoke**, we order double scotch, drain them, two
songs and no one has missed us. Feeling as though I have met my match

gunslinger liar inscrutable thrillseeker, it has always sounded like this —

It can't be wrong when it feels so right: Because the Night Belongs to
Lovers seeps into the backseat we have ignored — all night our only chance
to meet him, because the night covers us, long before Love is an Angel

it is cruel and left-handed,

singing the words in another language, summoning the day.

                        When we walk through the Market the sun is bright
                        Pain and pleasure unite us, walking past VIVE

He tells me **the only thing a gambler needs is a suitcase and a trunk.**

60

Packs his clothes so neatly, they are like crescent rolls. And pops
them in the drawer I have marked **M**:

a Peter Lorre film about compulsion, that it cannot be helped.

Western Hospital (Bathurst and Dundas) 1989–

. . . when things decay, it's not a sign of something gone wrong —
not in nature's grand scheme of things. It's a sign that nature is
reclaiming energy and materials that seem to be no longer needed
by higher organisms.
— Boyce Rensberger

Some things I remember I would like to forget:

blood soaks the inside of his thighs 3 A.M., the way the street
always looks at this hour on this ride;

the arc of Bathurst opening into emergency;

inert ambulance, waiting to sleep;

then he is staggering through the corridor while I confiscate
syringe, tie, and spoon;

watching his heart pulse in weak, secret spikes;

how he tried to die.

When I was afraid, I couldn't sleep. I would say,
I'm thinking you're going to die. I won't, everything's alright,
our hands linked;

sleep through this another time, going under the doctor asked me
to count backwards, like you can recover this; bitch;

murderer. Drawers filled with plastic bracelets, unusual bleeding
I want to forget this and more,

the mist that descends each time I make this trip.
Moving through vapour and blank space, walking the floor,
expecting morning.

Xtraordinaire (722 Queen Street West) 1994–96

I have never had a hairdresser before but things come to this.
Hand-carved crosses, piercing, face-slaps, lipliner.
He fits my hair with extensions, someone else's hair,

twice now, I wear this stranger's remains. My head scraped raw
with sutures, I sleep on my face, some fall out I am falling apart.

You look like a mermaid, Sook-Yin says when she sings to me.

He tells me about an associate, Ray, who almost died from fluorocarbons,
his aurora of hairspray, and leaves me under the dryer
while I think about glamour.

How angry 1 have been, lethal shoes talons corsets, you got to move on,
if you want to see glory, train train.

That glamour may be something else, walking slowly and painfully,
so there are no mistakes. The discomfort, the drag.
Of effacing yourself; the sublimation. Of recovering the grotesque.

I wonder at the hair of the skeleton, in museum glass, pulling a comb
through my own tangled *memento mori*.

I fought with my hairdresser once, viciously. Pretend I'm dead,
I told him, and slammed down the phone. Before we made up and since,
I think this is the most glamorous thing I have ever done:

his clips clattering to the floor — the nerve of that woman — my hair
alight, as I turn in an outrage, switching beauty's tail, to get moving.

Y yz

Three Triplets: Toronto — Guelph, 1996

progress / gets / lost in / the / trail of . . .

— Clifton Joseph

Early October, Cronenberg's **Crash** premieres & Amber Clifton Michael &
I meet on Dovercourt; bill has declined to join us, thinking we'll die in the
car: coming to meet us, Michael escaped an accident, head-on, two semi-

trucks cleaved ahead, swerving from the crush & fire he's shaken he
might turn thirty in a morgue. The highway yawns & we smooth-sail
tap through *The Israelites* like bonnies & clydes until the line seizes,
stopping dead, a crash — we wait in blue twilight,

for two hours until the smashed trailer is cleared from sight. Big rigs circle
the scene in elephantine grief; we are washed in red light, then banished.
We track the side road, genuine grace outfiies our need to cramp in love or
fear, to find the prayer that prefigures collision.

> later Esta & I will decide to be Millie & Chili
> & tour the Prairies
>
> Clifton screams Monk is Dead & cries
>
> Michael opens presents: we sonnetize
> (our pretty room).

Zoo (Metropolitan Zoo, 1984)

hog, big as a cannon,
how sweet yon lie.

— Anne Sexton

I am finishing a thesis on Anne Sexton, exhibiting *a disturbing insensitivity to paragraphs,* sophistry, mixed metaphors. It has taken seven years.

A poet who was *born doing reference work in sin,* and born confessing that in the end she is *a drunken rat.*

My high priestess of Quaalude and coffee, highballs for breakfast, her typewriter an altar, even then. A terrible poem before dying, her mind still moving in revolutions — long ago having realized that it was Eve who lay down with flowers

a Persephone-wreath of daisies in her hair — she plants these seeds, something seminal, about men and animals, long before there are gunshots and all girls off the pigs,

Janet and I visit the zoo. It is early spring and most of the exhibits are closed. One rhinoceros on a platform, wedged tight. A white tiger in a small cage, two giraffes kissing.

There is nothing to say about animals, I try to keep this in mind, wondering how poets lose their art. If compression and allusion come to disgust you, if it is cold and there are lions looking sick on a half-hill,

you may find that life is cruel and prosaic. Shudder, and say this: I watched a female gorilla. She stared at me through the plexiglass barrier as if she hated me. Then threw up in her hand and ate it. Never breaking eye contact.

We quiver like chicken binds . . .

Before the putrid ugliness, of everything we contain.

64

   The Black Knight, The Silver Rail, the Van by the River, Mary's Lysander, Star & Monika, The Brass Rail, Mildred Pierce, Ludwig-Vaughan, the Cayenne Pepper King, Nights in White Satin, College Street Fear, Extraordinary Erin, the Corner Pocket, Fright Nights, Love Empyreal, 717 Richmond West, The Werewolf, Etta James & KISS, Chopsticks & Traffic, The Waverly, the seahorse, the day

Miss Pamela's Mercy

Look Homeward, Angel
for Farrah Fawcett

I drink the cold black tea and Fatima holds
the cup with her left hand.
I watch her fingers
as she swirls the flowered enamel;
they are long roots clutching a peeled bulb,
crossed like plastic scissors with a jewelled fulcrum.
She collects rings: they shine on her hands and toes.
One is a gold filigreed heart
that hinges open to show a secret casket.
She keeps rat poison in there,
and lumps of blue drain powder.
Sometimes it is like a band of lizards
are creeping from her batwing sleeve.
Leashed with bright collars,
skimming coffee jars and milk jugs,
dusting them with pollen.
1 have seen lesions on the manager's lips,
and faint spots bleach his angry face.
She is killing him, she says,
with a hundred swords.
They clang in their small menace
when she drops the cup to the table.
She sees a crown in the tea leaves.
Four spires and a broad band;
it means a powerful friend will come to help me.
The number eight then curls
its swan neck around the dark mulch.
I will become more independent.
I feel the ache behind my shoulder blades
where three grey feathers hang.
Stitched into a blood-caked tangle

of knots and moulting skin.
The friend will be the man,
the man I become here,
when I turn into a gorilla.

I work in Henrietta, Oklahoma,
where my mother is from. I came here aimlessly,
finding her eyes in the road signs;
scraps of her pyjamas fly in the windstorms,
streaked cottonseeds.
I answered an ad for the carnival,
and thought it might help my acting
— to remember swallowing fire
or walking a tightrope along a cool empty skyline.
Instead, I was the featured attraction
in the enclosed burlap tent.
People came to watch thick animal hair
burst from my tender skin,
to see my serene face turn into scowling leather.
The man with pins in his cheeks and neck
speaks to me in a low whisper.
I nod from the cage, adjust my bikini,
and suddenly, horribly, catch on fire.
The swimsuit peels in a ribbon of flame,
pulling a skin of thorns across me.
My eyes boil, I growl and rip at
the bars.
The lights drop then, when the pierced man
leads me from the stage,
beyond the blurred blank faces.

I spend most of my time with Fatima,
in her tent of embroidered moons,
that drags like a tattered hem
along the dirty fairground.
I set her hair in pincurlers and rollers

while she stares moodily at her crystal ball.
I wondered what she saw in there,
I had always imagined
it was a spectral television,
where ghosts push their hollow limbs
against the curve of the glass,
writing threats in viscous ink.
She says she goes into a trance when she looks into it.
It is a chilly moon, beached in white sea sand,
a pink shell, clasping a pearl.
It is really her pupil,
a sightless black hole
in the dry creased earth.

And she feels the bumps on my head,
finding portents there,
scars and rips of light.
I tell her that Lee cut my hair off one day
in April when I was sleeping under the dryer,
dreaming about Ryan.
My husband told him to watch me,
as if I was an oil painting,
a cosmetic sun.
We fell in love instead.
He had hairdo dolls of me lined up into rows,
their target eyes shadowed in oily rainbows.
This love is buried
by the purple tide where I left him.
The fat wire rolls of my hair
tumble to the floor, severed by flashing metal bites.
They extend tawny feelers,
and hover in the stucco firmament
of our sky-black ceiling.
I see myself still,
framed by a corona of lightbulbs,
sheared to the scalp.

He smashed my statues
and tore up my photographs.
I am an Orpheus in diamonds,
on my hands and knees
picking up pieces of myself.

Her voice is a heavenly belt;
a zodiac that moves and hypnotizes me.
My thoughts leak; the beads of sugar
on the flat mouths of wedding cake boxes.
When I put it under my pillow
I dreamed I had lived in a laboratory
filled with cages and cauldrons.
The skin of the rats pulled off easily,
but I can't breathe when their ridged tails
tighten around my neck,
leaving a pendant of sewer water.
Fatima says it means I have lost a friend.
Little claws in my head.
The faint rustle of eyelet as I left the chapel,
an angel's wing made of baby's breath,
pinned in a blood-stained scrapbook.

Her lodestone nudges my scalp
as she raises my memories,
all of the dead.
My torn impressions stumble up,
are prodded with her magic wand.
Her crimson smile is a bewitching ointment
to my chills and fever,
a compelling powder,
a spell-breaking incense.
She burns it in a mojo bag
when I walk through the woods to the water,
naming trees and flora, and making the world begin.
I see his face in its sheer blue dress.
He frowns, wishing I would return.

He concentrates on the three coffins,
of lead, pewter, and ivory.
My hair waves inside,
filaments of seaweed curve like hot magma;
my lava mouth and volcanic eyes.
His hesitation is the peaceful space
around me, here by the shore where
I reach up starfish arms to hold
the night's rich flannel sleeves.

There are vultures in the air,
whose tufted chins wave as they ascend.
They surround me tonight,
as I fasten my hooks and clasps,
dropping bones on the rocks,
and beating their veined tailfeathers.
I wait in the spotlight,
listening to the tin jungle music.
The painted drums and lions' paws,
panting vines and arms of bracelets.
My friend fumbles with his ape head,
and pats my hand.
I see his rubber palm cover mine,
and think fleetingly of my monstrous head,
a silicone temple, a hanging garden.
The crashing skull of Anne Boleyn,
the girl of Linwood, Kansas.
She copied my hair,
and on Valentine's Day, her friend poured
nitric acid on her scalp.
The hated mass slid to the floor,
like blonde love potion.
Her neck and shoulders blaze,
her collar of burns.
Her head, when I touch it, is the prim lace
rimming red velvet.

I hear someone scream
when the lights dim;
the screen slowly moves down,
covering me with a film
of simian limbs and furled violet lips.
I slip back into the dressing room,
and realize that it is time for me to leave.
The orange fall is here,
my hair hangs to my shoulders
in long yellow plumes.
I erase my face
with brilliant makeup,
and ask Fatima to arrange a party.
She promises to sew me a gown,
from the tarot Empress,
who walks softly,
brandishing an ornate sceptre.

A strapless formal with an orchid corsage,
phalanged chiffon,
that fills the room
as we bow our heads to the seance.
A candle flickers when she asks my life
to come forward, to possess her voice.
At first, there is only laboured breathing,
but then a static squall begins,
and her face melts into a collage.
Lee chastises me,
and Ryan's tongue splits and pleads.
They tell me to come back,
they flush in shame for me.
In this swelling circle,
the fat man in the satin briefs,
the pinhead boy,
the gorilla,

the pinhead lady,
the snake charmer,
and me.

This group will recede,
a gem in a setting that I will
draw my courage from,
when I lie on my round waterbed,
covered by the gaudy armature
of their strength and beauty.
The voices stop,
are pulled like a sheaf of scarves,
a twitching rabbit from my ears.
And Fatima holds my face in her oracular hands
and speaks: "He which testifieth these things saith,
Surely I come quickly."
My eyes are wet, black
cygnet hoods, but even so,
I look homeward with her.

The Black Dahlia

The doorman at the Biltmore
watches the moon quake.
It glows and sinks, a bright fissure
in the dark broadcloth,
and the Black Dahlia
walks by.
Her murky hair is huge,
a perennial mass on a dusky stalk.
She moves through the grey mist
and into his tender arms.
He binds her wrists and ankles
with rope as she droops
from her weight.
And winter days pass as he clips
her foliage, saving slender shoots
washing the grubs
from her pallid leaves.

The child screamed when she saw her,
cut in half that way.
Scattered in the field
in gleaming pieces,
cored into two white husks.
Her hair, coloured scarlet,
streaming over her battered skull,
and her eyes like comets,
shine through blood.

I back away
from the welter of lesions,
the constellation of keratoid scars,
the pentacle carved from her thigh,
where a rose tattoo bloomed.

It's stuffed in the abyss
of her tortured body,
its pink arms pried shut.

She sprawls along my bed this fall,
her roots growing through
the parched Saltillo sheets.
Her mouth is cut into a purple slash,
she toils and spins;
her hatred rocks the marble angels.
I sew her together
with needles and pins,
and strip her hair back, blue and black.
We grow a rose in the windowsill,
and plant it in the triangular gap.
She chooses agate marbles
and sets them in her hollow sockets,

Elizabeth — she takes me by the hand.
To visit him, the faceless gardener.
He stands tending rows of flowers.
Consumed by burning red
and orange petals, he cuts and prunes.
His hands are lustrous,
pricking thorns,
scorpions from the soil.
She is radiant as she leaps,
and drives the stake
through his blistered heart.
And we climb
the ladder of his ravaged flesh,
past the sulphurous gates and home.
Where she leaves me,
to pass into the ephemera,
and stare cruelly from the sky.

Carrie Leigh's Hugh Hefner Haiku

Hef brings me flowers
tiger lilies, ochre veined
downcast, sleek black cups

small shadows, are the
puckers in his pyjamas
where his skin caves in

tired profligate, I
sigh and pour the oil along
your circular sheets

thinking of all the
times, or women on this bed,
glossy old bunnies

I imagine their
breasts, plate of fried eggs, a row
of tonsured monks' heads

his tongue slithers, gaunt
voluptuary, ugly
old man, my eyes close

when I roll his name
Ner along my tongue, like the
line of cold test tubes

thin bottled semen
he wants to plant it, deeply
in my flat belly

named Hugh Junior, or
Carietta, a child is
packed in dry blue ice

in silk pyjamas
they have an emperor's crest,
it is dark in there

but it's as cold as
the green Jacuzzi, bubbles
are clouds on its face

1 will crush the glass
with the fingers in his back
and pile on my rings

and all the fur coats
and move down the circular
stairway, thick with gold

the flowers are a
Venus flytrap, with red curls
flames and noxious breath

his betrayal gives
me granite fists, girls scatter
movie stars crumple

as I run away,
from the gaudy prison cell,
of tinsel and skin

I'll sue him and write
and build a home, deep in the
desert, on the sun

a sequined Venus,
a mirage — in loungewear and
harlequin glasses

Miss Pamela's Mercy
for Pamela Des Barres

When Michael left me,
I gave him a gift of grace.
For the silk garters,
emerald and lapis lazuli.
The orange cameo —
my hair layered into suns
and two Madonnas —
my title, the Marquise Des Barres.
I left him the glass bottles,
the buttonhooks and tap shoes.
My holy relics, the Judas lips,
the saint's fingers I kissed.
Tonight I am a scientist,
with a crate of kings and archbishops.
The girl in the pink satin
bustier, who will only dance
when Iron Butterfly is playing.
She throws long yellow roses,
and pulls at Daryl's zipper
with her teeth.
The shadow in the cemetery,
backlit with purple haze.
I wanted to write a moral story,
even though I married a vicious man.
His glitter and plastic
tool kit, his velvet platforms.
My tender heart,
notorious and threadbare.

He started writing poetry
near the end.
Early in the morning,
his mascara streaked

and hair in pincurlers.
I would scramble eggs with
cheese while he read lines like
I'm so ill,
There are black stitches on my wrists.
He said Byron and Verlaine were
glamorous men, with pale
skin and ruffled collars,
square-cut cufflinks, long jet
curls.
He shudders,
knows he is gifted.
The ones he loves are dead.
He says their images torment his sleep,
he is burning.
Pamela, what do you think, or do
you see what I'm doing here.
He reads me long fractured
poems about heroin.
I want people to see its duality
he says, a dialectic, and
says I wouldn't understand.
There are books I should read,
he tells me, this is what a caesura is.
It is something between us.
I put some space there.

I wrote to Mercy.
She lives in a silver trailer in Lake County,
where Johnny Burnett drowned.
I asked about the blues society
and said I needed her.
I was nervous
waiting with Michael and his friends,
pasting pictures to playing cards
and writing below.

A doll's esophagus, this is pressed angel hair.
They drew something called
a beautiful corpse
with three blind panels.
They handwashed their wool turtlenecks
and rope sandals,
they said I was Helen of Troy.

Paris shaves his eyebrows into diagonal slits
and wears scorpions,
Osiris medallions,
gold-plated, signs.
I hear the spirit
Paris calls the god of the dead,
its sleek feather head and shining eyes,
circling the necropolis.
His hands unwrap the linen from my ribs,
he recites tantras from my diary.
About my other life, a sheer slip
tacked with stars and planets.

We met when Mercy and Lucky/Jinx
who is her son with Sugie
went down to the river.
We basted catfish and cracked
oysters on the rocks,
sultry night, the moon a paper plate
in the hot sky.
I remember my violin
and first visit here,
when I prayed in the rain forest
and Aunt Mildred sang
Safe am I in the hollow of His hand.
Who heard me
as clear as if I were shouting,
who listens still.

When Paris asks which of the three
I would choose if I could,
their cold hands brush
my neck.

And Jimmy appears
in his Aleister Crowley cape
with the white ribbon and red cross,
like magic.
If I close my eyes I am with him.
I watch from the amplifier
with their turquoise bracelets
heavy on my arm.
He smiles
and Robert falls to the floor
on his knees.
His golden hair singed with spotlight,
he sings O *let the sun heat down upon my face.*
Jimmy's palms on the strings,
this wet violence.
His whips sliding
into the flowered wastebasket.
And the bruise
he pulled from my neck
with his cruel lips.
Desperate for him,
I sewed him a rodeo shirt.
Long peach fringes,
pricked with cowskull
and cactus thorns,
I wrote him a love song that ended,
Come in from the storm / Come
Inside.
My lace corset,
my sorrow.

She dusted my face
with pink rice powder,
Beverly, my belladonna.
She is frail and monarch orange.
When I cried to her about my loss,
she held me in the plush
of her arms.
Her lisle sleeves
spreading like a prayer mat,
the veiled windows.
Her beauty is the heaven of art, my fetish.
She would burn hair and skin
on a stick of violet charcoal —
High John the Conqueror —
his armour of pearl and nightshade,
her melancholy.
Printing hexes with a carved potato,
her track-marks livid and virgin blue.
She slips into joy, with faith and
my devotion.
Her pencil thin moustache and smile
when I walked down the aisle
and married her.
I saw the halo of my first sacrament,
when *I dreamed of a life*
that was pure and true.

Before I fell (into the big
sleep) that torrid night with Jim,
I called his profile the triumph of Jupiter.
I am the lizard king, he said,
I can do anything.

His hand on my thigh
is aqua regia, corrosive,
as we drive through La Brea,

inhaling Trimar from cotton scraps.
He sees scales and tusks
sinking into the dull surface
of the tar pits.
The gas and Stardust,
the fire when he kissed me.
His celestial tongue, cherry red.
Half insane, he imagined tiny monsters,
and his lonely descent.
Below the grey bathwater,
surprised, extinct.
I see the frill of his hair,
his flesh, spiked and dangerous,
eclipsed by my rash desire,
and sweet in my mouth.

Paris hands me the Earth, undivided.
Love's geography, ragged and wild.
I tell him about Danceland,
as we walk along the shore,
through the clay and milkweed.
I was a b-girl there,
swaying under the prisms
of a silver sun,
as a broken man
proposed to me.
Will you be
the diamond he offered,
hopeful and strange.
The facets of devotion
in your dark narrow eyes.
I fold this metaphor
into an envelope for Michael.
And my friend Mercy pulls me into the lake,
we cross over when she baptizes me.

Goodnight, Goodnight
for Hervé Villechaize

Your dress is too tight for you.
The holes cut in the side
reveal an angry flux of skin
that bulges like the birth of an oracle.
The printed pyramids are stretched,
as if they are housing an ample Pharaoh,
and those yellow sphinxes look torpid and sick.
The night is here — you draw two watery triangles
on your brow, and walk away.
Heels scratching, waist splashing in, then out.
You are tall, alert on a staircase.
And I love the look of your black eyes
in the wet flower of your face.

You are polishing a rifle at home.
Its mouth yawns,
as you slither on the bed.
She is quiet in a chair when you ask for music.
A Latin dance,
your arms clamp her thighs in a blur.
You mesmerize her — with your pendulous larynx
and the bean brown plush of your throat.
And you tell her about a summer you spent in France,
to work on a painting.
It was a great achievement, this heroic portrait.
You modelled all day as Napoleon,
and your hands were cramped from their seclusion.
They feel rough and matted, a surprise
on the edge of two dimpled baby's arms.

She keeps phoning in a teary voice
that is dulled with devotion.
And asks about your lover.

I say that he tore the dress from you angrily
and you sprawled along the pavement.
That he lived with giraffes,
and that he bought you things.
I see you wear them sometimes
like careless reminders, the time
when your heavy skirt parted,
and showed off silver bracelets.
She pines, and sharpens her pencil.
In a steady hand writes,
they won't find me, to you.
A violent wind disturbs your lipstick.
Its bright red shows you,
dancing a two-step, dusky hair upon hair
in a blizzard of beauty.

Jacobina Willhemina Carman
1973–87

to Mary

At fourteen, she could be wearing black,
her skin is the silver of clouds and seraphim.
She leaves in the rain, her dappled head turned,
and her blue eyes, now jewelled with mascara,
are a receding diadem.
She slides like soap in the bath, and sleeps with me,
found shot to death in a ditch in Bentinck Township, on side road 5.

The holes in her rib and cheek pucker,
like rotted fruit. My nightmare's fingers pick at it,
try to pull out the sliver of gold from where it flames.
And hold the heart turned rusted,
rimmed orange on slate grey,
an inert sunset — sunk low and silent.
Her limbs tangled in the dirt, hair rain-torn and wild.
Growing back into the earth, the roots surge,
pushing spears and bulbs through her bloodless frame.
They lift her gently with black gloves,
press her staring eyes closed.
I feel the pulse of their stasis, and the beat of the gun.

The most beautiful name
I could think of, torn from fiction.
A Jacob's ladder of syllables coursing across my stomach.
A name to evoke a captive genius,
and to stir her amniotic heart.
And Carmen playing, as I dance,
clumsy in my pregnancy,
with a rose in my teeth. The petals I chewed on,
their veins seductive, their colour sweet.
She comes out with her forehead pleated and crimson —
and her still wet body a trembling stem.

I would try to write you an elegy, about being
thrown back into the loam of Ayton,
to seed the soil and sky with fragments of your eyes.
But I can only think of questions,
that end with the simplicity, of you choosing, say,
your pineapple barrette, or green scarf,
and walking into the night.
Without an aria, rising to meet you in grief,
just driving with the wind and radio,
and playing pool and meeting someone
I will never know.

I try to capture this man: he walks beside me,
unblinking. Faces come to me, a rogues' gallery.
Mild mouths clamped over vicious teeth,
and eyes with tombstone pupils.
Or thin hands that held onto fingers,
and toss rifles carelessly into closets.
The man that kept you prisoner,
when I dreamed of you, over fourteen years ago.

The pictures you drew
still rustle around the house, are pinned to the walls.
Drawings of you,
as a child in a yellow playsuit,
its big feet poking through the crib slats.
A girl asleep in my arms on the beach;
on your last day of school, your hand
on your hip, blonde hair tangled and smiling lips.
Your life stops, and this glow seeps through.
Like watching your pale lungs burst and begin the universe.
The silence of my days, I leave you,
with the books closed, and Carmen dead.

VillainElle

Saturday Night Fever

I'm going nowhere
  somebody help me
  somebody help me there

His white suit a peerless lily
the wide lapels an allegorical breastplate.
The *Prima Porta Augustus,*
his arm-divine is raised to the glittering ceiling.
    I am the little cupid that clings to
    his thigh — symbolizing Venus, Venus
Goddess of love that I am. When he holds me and we dance,
my cool silk dress skims my thighs, arouses me and I am
more than a woman,
    more than a woman when I defile his neck,
his spotless collar with coral — the pink skeleton:
my lips are jewellery, but as my body pushes closer,
he moves, elegantly, easily, from me

There are two kinds of girls — and nice girls don't —
    push him into the car. Joey and Double J
dangerous, circling outside. His gold chains are hot on
    my breastbone —
white bliss when he pushes my skirt higher, higher — *heaven,*
and stops: *just give me a blow job.*

That night I experienced love, not love, wanting
all of him; he looks away, wanting more.

The Brooklyn Bridge, a temple-icon at his throat.
I see his dreams are hopeless, small, and still, I follow him.

To the hardware store, and finger nails screws rakes.
I want him to brush my body with plaster of Paris, cool enamel paint,
until I am pale, bridal, the tender moon.

To show him that there are *sublunary lovers,* that there is
nothing between his fine chalk suits, his blue work smock:
mutability and constancy: there are spheres, turning endlessly
in the skies. Where angels sing in *a harmony of ravishing beauty.*

I decide to sleep with him instead, there is a selection of
         condoms in my hand when I reach for him
outside the 2001 — he slaps them to the ground,
         as if I am alien, clinical, devouring, and walks,
indifferent to longing, space.

Bobby is pacing the sidewalk, in perilous platforms, crying
call me Tony, call me — are you going to call me Tony?

I am plotting revenge, a night of abandon, near oblivion,
I do not recognize him, myself.

Envying his power, despising his weakness,

the car is idling when Tony approaches, his face is
         battered, still lovely, his life is changing this night.
I drink moonshine from a flask and lay down between his
         friends as we drive, strange tongues, teeth assail me.
He asks, *Are you happy, are you happy now?* His disgust
         is a tonic.

I close my eyes at the whiteness
the glare of their exposed underwear, I imagine

they are vulnerable, that I dictate their
yearning: *how deep is your love,* your love.

I thought I wouldn't cry, it felt like something,
something better than

loneliness, anguish: Bobby is climbing the golden spires
of the bridge

exultant and desperate, he is showing them, he is showing me
that there are times

when your chest splits and separates and there is your heart.
Broken, beating, there are such terrible miracles.

His body demolished beneath the water, my screams
exalting him.

I let them lead me away, because they are afraid, but it is this:
the sweet descent of his dauntless body,
the healing black water, a dark coronet
that bears him below and carries him, it carries me to safety.

Betty and Veronica

Today was a day like any other,
I stayed in my room and burned incense —
love me fairy cones — and dreamed
about Veronica. I saw her black hair,
its streaks — *lapis lazuli* — in the
crown of ash. I thought jealously
of her small hands in his,
of the squash-coloured stains
at the nape of her neck.
Where his cold lips embellished
her beauty.
His ankles are pale beneath the vine,
the abrasions are cactus flowers, scorpions,
these shapes corrupt her memory.
I saw her when she kneeled beside him,
held her veil against him and Veronica

irons her religion to her sleeves and pockets.
His sorrowful face is golden, luminous,
a decal on each *ensemble*. She laminates
every tear with clear nail polish and
tells me I know nothing about love.
She says these are *the days of vengeance,*
and is suspended when she throws stones
through the classroom windows.
I want to kiss her, I am desperate,
but she denies me this betrayal.
I am reduced to staring at my idol,
when she passes me in the streets.
Once, I saw her at a perfume counter,
spraying her wrists with an atomizer of Shalimar.
Her serene eyes were clouded with mystery

and that night I left lilies on her doorstep.
Her delicate feet are a garland of flowers,
a string of pearls in platform sandals, an altar.

I pin my prayers to a photograph of her.
She is burning money and her arms
are spread open, she is bleached
by the light of the sun.
I pray she will come to me tonight and bless
my body with her hot breath and cruel mouth.
I am lost inside of her, as her spirit
becomes flesh, generous and sweet.
I hear her walking in the grass, circling
the garden below.
She calls to me to join her
and tells me how she hates me.
His impression, soulful and cryptic,
rejects me too, but I reach for her still,
for her faithless heart,
and we fall to the earth,
struggling, and wild with desire.

Strange Fits of Passion

for Xaviera Hollander

Strange fits of passion have I known:
And I will dare to tell,
But in the Lover's ear alone,
What once to me befel.

— William Wordsworth

I lick my lover's ear and it burns
as my tongue traces the lobe, helix, ossiculum.
His hands reach for the ribbons,
the snap-panel of my edible underpants;
he wants to taste the sugar, its sweet fruit centre.
He moans as I slap his hands
away; as I unclasp my tiger-skin bustier,
my red ruffled garter,
and I slide my stockings slowly
past my thighs, knees, and ankles.
I ask him to strip and gaze as he
peels away his vest, his nylon socks,
his mesh briefs and stands
nervous and hopeful, before me.
Now dance, I say,
in these manacles and restraints.
I sway my silver hair to the mariachi songs
and the radio plays into the hot evening
as he turns and spins
and listens.

This happened to me when I was
a madam and I never told a soul.
But I confessed everything else:
the baleful eyes of the German
shepherd that licked my thighs
and raked me with his saffron paws,

the boy whose come tasted like clotted cream,
the first girl I ever kissed when I was a child
and her nipples were pastille-sweet
in my mouth.
I was beautiful then, the sky
was my replica, cheekbone steeples
and the mist of my moonlit hair.
I was making breakfast for my girls,
in a gingham apron and bonnet.
Pofferties, little puff pancakes,
and *ontbijtkoek.*
Anna was brushing the pans with melted butter,
her fingers were shining translucent
and I saw the sun burn against
the depressions in the metal.
I reached out and touched the soft
wildflowers, the sleeves of her nightgown.
She held me in her arms
and we kissed below the picture window
where the glass panes shook
and the tulip bulbs trembled in their pots.
And all the saints came, with pastry dolls and potato parings
wrapped in paper and string.
We cut them open and found the red
inlaid stones inside, we wore them
in our navels as we walked, slowly,
up the stairs, our clothes drifted
to the landing, our hands
bound with a delicate web.
As we ascended, I watched the sun
drop into the poplars and my heart beat,
faster, it constricted in my chest.
I turned to her and saw
her face, radiant in the light
as the cruel branches reached and
devoured the sun and I cried,

I screamed, if Anna should be dead!
She murmurs quietly into the night
and bathes my face with cool water,
witch hazel. But I am inconsolable,
I stare at the stars and I understand.
For it is written there, I tell him,
all of it. There is my body, holy,
luminous, and there is the space,
the impression of Anna, of Anna lost
against me. Her eyes were white and still,
her lips bled as we parted.
The storm clouds, the bruises on her battered face.
He resembled you, I said,
he had your desire.

He was quiet also, and I whipped him,
I ground my heels in his chest
until he begged for mercy.

Poems for Jack the Ripper

i. He Also Serves Who Only Stands and Waits

And somehow you asked me to stay
But not to ask why
No not to ask why

I have never discovered your identity,
although we were very close once.
There were several clues,
a scraping of skin,
the atlas of scars beneath
the tissue on my chest.
At the time, I asked you
about the others and you said,
What does it matter when you're the one 1 love?
You could be tender, pulling
me close when I screamed,
and in the orange of your nightgown
I was enveloped by the moon.
But sometimes I am afraid.
When the shadows fall,
in long slivers in the mist,
and your feet creep in the corners, in the black
edges of the night, a rustle of dead leaves and pale white bone.
You have returned,
unknown, to these narrow streets.
My heart is a bad neighbourhood,
its tenements lie derelict, condemned.
To remember you, to feel your
cold fingers closing my eyes
once more.

She is almost a wraith,
she is not apparent.
Her green eyes are luminous,

the clockface that glows as I lay awake,
turning. I have seen this colour before,
a sick jealous glare.
A thorn in my side when I asked you,
again and again, where you were,
the night before.
Your surgical gloves run pink under the tap,
you look dishevelled and wild.
You said I was suspicious, you said terrible things:
Why don't you kill yourself?
I had let myself fall apart, and she,
she is frail and pitiless,
her hair is lace, wormwood
and there is bile flowing sweetly
from her lips.

I sensed that things were not right,
the crimson ink blotted on mysterious envelopes,
the newspaper, sliced to ribbons.
I saw you dreamily folding
flour and kidney into a pie shell,
and you smiled.
You looked strangely beautiful
as you placed it before me.

I had written, urgently,
privately, *God help me,*
and I came to regret this.
Your surveillance was exhaustive,
and I cried the night I burned my letters.
You made a mark on my forehead with the ashes,
you left that night, and I waited by the window, anxious,
contrite. When the light broke through the shutters,
I heard you, heavy on the stairs.
I heard the bloodhounds too, and the grieving sirens.
There was no sign of resistance,

she held her arms benevolently
to the bitter sky.
I have no malice, no wisdom to give her,
because I could not resist him.
His hate, his cruelty pulls like a stone,
and I fall, beneath the dark water,
of seduction.

ii. I Prayed in Whitechapel

I fell to the floor
of the white chapel, at the altar
in late October.
The icy wind rattled the clerestory windows,
where the sun bleaches his sorrowful face.
My god is delinquent, his eyes clamped shut
as a procession of children,
dressed as witches, lizards,
sunflowers, files solemnly below.
A girl in white tulle touches my hand with a paper star
and I shake with nausea.
The tile floor is cool
against my cheek, I am dreaming.
He is carving pumpkins in the gaslight,
their dreadful smiles are uneven,
burning. He is listening to Tosca,
with the sound turned low:
Ecco vedi, e merce d'un tou detto,
I implore him to speak to me.
The point of the knife shines
as it disappears,
into the pocket of his overcoat.
His shoes, his shirtsleeves are pocked with brilliant red.
It's part of my costume, he explains to me;
I am wearing a disguise.
He pulls a stocking over his face

and stares through its sliced foot-seam.
Don't wait up, I will be quite late.
The pumpkin bread is warm
in the oven, for his return.
My nails are coated with the slippery rind,
and I bite them, nervously,
as I rise to leave.

iii. Remorse

Sometimes, when I am cleaning
the broken glass and splinters,
the gale of his temper,
he looks remorseful.
He says, *I can't seem to help myself.*
He would be reading in the basement —
Tales from the Crypt —
and his father would find him
and beat him with a leather belt,
and burn the horror comics in the backyard.
He remembers the weird green haze,
of the fire, watching their paper faces,
powerless, as the unkind orange
effaced them.
He heard his mother playing the organ, mournfully,
from a distance, *How Great Thou Art.*
He sees the stars,
he hears the roar of thunder,
forever in his temples, beating.
And he is still, after the anger passes.
I smooth the damp hair from his forehead,
and he clutches a faint rag doll
to his chest. He traces its mouth, a line
of yarn stitches and cries,
the tears fall like comets
from its button eyes.
He says, *I wish all things were alive.*

iv. The Miracle Fish

She places the fortune-telling fish,
a sliver of red cellophane,
on her palm. Its tail turns over:
False, she is untrue to me.
She crumples it and it is motionless
when I touch it: *Dead One.*
She loves symmetry, deception,
her voice is the light rustle,
the bat whispers,
her bed is papered
with gift wrap, mash notes.
I recognize his signature, a cloak and dagger;
I look away, her silence
is beguiling, emerald grass,
the burnished earth of my grave.
I relinquish this delirium
because I need courage.
To love her, although she is also deadly,
such thorns in my skin.
She asks for my blessing,
and receives it.
Passion flowers
arrayed brightly on her wedding gown.
I am streaming petals
behind her as she walks,
each apostle glows in the violet night.
The air is sweet with pollen,
and he is breathless when he looks beyond me
at her glorious approach.

v. Few Are Left Unafraid of the Phantom Killer

He left suddenly, and never returned,
but he is still out there.

I hear him, the cautious step,
the spin of the grindstone.
He was careful, meticulous;
he placed my rings and hair-
pins in a circle, as I slept.
My vanity, he said, a dubious halo.
The knife inches closer to my neck,
he is sallow, malevolent,
telling me to die,
I hate the sight of you, walking the street.
Running to escape him,
I fall down and he steps on my
arms and cuts me.
I'm not what you think, I tell him,
choking on blood and panic,
but it's hopeless, he overcomes me,
a viridian wave, and slices his name,
deep, in my heart.
Where it blisters and flames,
he kisses me, coldly —
I hear *Murder* in the echoes —
and he promises me,
we will meet again.

The Chicken-Baby

A car radio bleats,
"Love, O careless Love. . . ." I hear
my ill-spirit sob in each blood cell

— Robert Lowell

Jack and I were fighting —
he threw knives and flames over my head
and they sailed to the floor below us.
The fire began there, in the Ministry of Love.
Because there were no windows,
he explained, and we were slow,
the glow of little sunsets: Valium,
this was lovely and calm. Yellow,
burning, his voice was always sweet.
Golden veins, threading the intemperate earth;
I slashed at his arms, his ankles,
as we left; I renewed myself
with these riches.

He was a vision in sky blue,
and I was converted. I saw signs and wonders
I did not believe.
Light, flowing from the gas-elements.
In the cold night,
the ants and silverfish moved in careful circles
and we were quiet as the rain beat
against the ceiling glass.
This was long before he became remote and I became dangerous.
He worked, very briefly, as a sailor
and I slept with my hands in the waves.
I lay like a message in the sand,
waiting for his safe return.

He turned away because his bones ached,
and I looked at the anatomy of his accidents.
Shadows, pain, in the interstices
between flesh and metal.
He cries out in his dreams, when I trouble these spaces,
when I push him, angrily, hard.
Helen, then, was my closest friend.
Her beautiful face was notorious;
she had caused anguish, destruction.
I was aware of her senseless grace,
the swan feathers that coronate her hair.
She is insidious, artless,
her eyes, her mouth a luscious error.
But her small affections
have left me defenceless,
as though my faith is latticework, filigree.
As though he knows this, he sings:
The fault is not mine, not mine.

My hands burn in their bandages.
Helen is nervous and unsure
when she tells me she loves him.
I tell her that he is
no longer of this world.
I have gathered what remains,
a brown envelope: letters, ribbon,
ash, a sepia picture.
He is alone, gesturing,
to the presents concealed in his pockets.
He was devoted to arcane objects, *chinoiserie.*
I remember, with pain, the chicken-baby.
Pink felt sleeper, orange eyes;
he placed it in my palm,
its voice a passionate squeak —
Love, O careless Love.

Nothing is ever demolished,
by fire, or history. When I
returned home, after his
furious departure, like a bride,
like a queen, it lay beheaded.
His absence is palpable now.
I have always been lonely,
he knew this and more.
That I would paste and sew each piece together.
That I would recognize him,
his frail likeness,
that flares like a miracle in everything
that is broken, and lost.

Corporal Punishment

I am troubled by his nightstick, his baton.
As if he were pressing it against my thighs,
his handcuffs snaking slowly around
my ankles.
His cropped hair is a bed of sweet grass
and his holster drops, in a clatter,
and burns at the foot of the bed.
When he cruises by me in the late afternoon,
I think he may arrest me
this time. Eventually,
somewhere, at a dance club,
he will sidle up to the bar
and offer me money.
When I reach for the flower of green and blue bills,
he will pull out his badge.
I will fix my lipstick in its bright reflection
and offer him my hands.
I have dressed carefully in garters,
seamed stockings, a rayon wig.
You bastard, I say, tenderly,
as he leads me to the backseat of the car.
The seat where the windows and doors won't open,
it is a dream, I am floating in space,
I am dying, in the compass, the space where his thumbprints
bruise my wrists.
My darling, I breathe into the ink pad, the camera.
Will you keep this on your dresser, querido?
And look at me, when you prick your fingers,
sewing your medals to your white shoulders,
you will tremble as the blood wells and hold me
closer, even closer —

My father was a car thief,
I remember the wire hangers in his suit pocket,
the hot wires.
He would sit and tattoo his chest and stomach
with food dye and a safety pin.
Pale red spark plugs, a pair of dice;
he told me about the long arm of the law,
touching my hair, through the branches
of the trees that framed my window,
combing it into a shining French roll.
In Paris, I walk with the corporal,
in a grey-and-white striped *chemise.*
He slaps me when he learns
I have been unfaithful and we drink cassis —
the blood of blackcurrants, heavy and sweet.
I take his pearl-handled revolver for target practice,
the tin cans on the fence, lychees in syrup,
are ragged with holes and flowing as I fire.
And fire, the polished metal of his abdomen
is brazen in the flames.
He calls my name, *Miranda,* and I shudder.

I embrace the pillows and sheets,
alone on my bed I reduce him.
My lover is the interval, inside the gun barrel.
He is the bore, the emptiness I devour
when I am hungry and in the mood for love.

Skirt, My Pretty Name

and the space between my name and myself grows larger until . . .
— David Demchuk, *Rosalie Sings Alone*

After several Valium and a cup of coffee, I
      feel sweet and contented. The city is dangerous,
prurient, and I am a woman of mystery. I ask
      the waitress for some napkins and whisper,
My husband's brains are in my hands. I ask her
      to regard the blood and tissue, the horror of my
dress. I am wearing tinted sunglasses, a chiffon
      scarf, patterned with lemons and cherries.
My wig, my hair is concealed, it really is awful,
      a cerise-coloured rat's nest and it itches, badly.
When I leave, I move smoothly through the streets,
      clutching my shopping bags; I fit my key into
the lock and gaze at my calling card, that reads:
      Skirt, my pretty name.

I am applying Lee press-on nails and listening to
      The Magic of Mantovani. I am having a nervous
breakdown, *You don't bring me flowers,* I remember
      coming home once and finding a sprig of lilacs
on my doorstep and I held them and *thought of him I love.*
      He was a merchant marine, and I was his
novitiate. I held conch shells to his ears
      while he slept, so he could hear the sea,
the sheets billowed like sails when he kissed me.
      He would powder my nose, he traced his fingers
down my thighs, *my flaw.* He was never, he was rarely cruel to me.
      When he left, I wore a mourning veil and sewed
starfish over my eyes. I cried like a siren, I slashed my
      wrists with a broken bottle. It lay on the carpet
shattered, with a silver ship in its neck.

Weeks in the hospital, without perfume, or candy,
        and I still have no friends. Yesterday, a man
came over to me and screamed about the accident,
        the blood! I shrank, smaller, into my sweater
and imagined I was somewhere else. The women in the
        restaurant smile when I take their pictures
with a pink Instamatic and offer them
        spoonfuls of chocolate, my number. I am staring
at the telephone now, willing it to ring, cradling it in my
        arms and my stomach is turning. I beat myself
with my fists, my loneliness is relentless. I see its constancy
        in the spreading bruises, the green and yellow echoes.
I am the quietest object here, I could rest here always, never moving.

Only breathing, the faintest shadow, slowly
        turning the pages of my library book,
Fashion in the 1970s, and naming the dances
        under my breath. I would step from side to side
and do the hustle, but I am tired and solemn.
        I am the light that jewels their white pantsuits;
the mirrored disco ball made of shattered stars.
        The dancers sway beneath me in an orbit
and sometimes stare, with a comb or a tissue.
        They see that they are broken, mortal,
and they look away.

He Scares Me So

I never thought I'd come to this . . .

My outfit, discarded on a chair, is a conversion narrative.
A tunic, imprinted with the Seven Seals; a rayon shirt
that depicts the moon landing.
Intrepid astronauts, placing little flags in violet craters.
I had rarely thought of Him since my confirmation,
but I remember the impression of His head,
on the pillow beside me, protecting me.
I am almost feverish as I drift
through the silent streets to the first
performance of Jesus Christ Superstar.

I am mad to oppose the stars, I see the bones of lost
friends, pure white, singing. There are angels in the snow
with coal black eyes and flowing skirts.
the psychedelic glow — blue sunshine — in my veins, my heart.
I am alone, anonymous when I watch the opera,
wild with sympathy. For Mary, *she has had so many men before;*
in very many ways, He's just one more.
I have also loved the likes of Him,
mysterious, distracted, His quickening rage.
He is screaming in the temple in a divine temper
and she consoles Him, *myrrh for His hot forehead, O.*
I am suddenly tired of consolation: I *understand what power is,*
understand what glory is.

It is, this time, the hulking figure of the Centurion
who averts his eyes and scourges Christ.
He brings Him to His knees
with a foot on His hem and the vinegar,
the tears are burning on my cheeks.
He is desirable to me even later, as he presses
through the crowd from the stage

and I move quietly behind him.
I slip my hand beneath his leather waistband
and touch the small of his back.
I want what you have, I tell him, in a perilous voice.
He misunderstands, and turns
and crushes me in his arms. He mashes his lips against
mine and I feel his mouth open, his tongue depresses
mine in one swift gesture. I rake my nails
down his neck until he cries out, furious.
As I walk home, I suck his blood from my fingers,
and wonder why he ruined everything; I think of gravity

annihilating the sky that evanesces above me,
there are pieces missing from my life, I know this.
And still I am confounded by science, the laws of attraction,
the apparent brightness of a star depends on two things:
how much light it radiates and how far it is,
how far it is from me.

I Am Curious (Yellow)

He is such a slut, he tells me he never
wears underwear. He gestures between his legs,
and I think of the cool air arousing him.
There is ice on the streets, ice like glass and I fell
(Oh God, I fell for you).
I brought him a pot of tulips, pink, tender,
barely blooming. He is unconscious of metaphor,
my desire is parenthetical, unseen.
As if I am undercover — the purple satin sheets
that cling to his thighs — I listen for clues
when he speaks.
I decipher his kiss: the bitter taste — small green apples,
his mouth is insistent, and I am breathless,
curious.
Yellow light filters through the keyhole,
he closes the door *(green with silver hinges)*
behind me, suddenly.
I am left alone with my thoughts of love,
my undeviating fictions.

His little rejections are stimulating;
he compounds what is mysterious, what is unknown:
a man loved wholly beyond wisdom.
Half sick of shadows, I compel myself to see him,
to see him for the first time.
There are amber scales on his crooked teeth;
once, I thought of golden scarabs, pressed gold leaf.
He told me he enjoyed hurting me, *I live for it,* he said.
I thought I was dead, I envied him that much.
With my head buried in my collar,
I begin to *undress him with my eyes.*
Each grey scrap — a worry bead —

his sad striptease bewitches me.
His pale flesh begins to emerge, his spine,
a fleet silhouette, a lizard, distressed.
He is mortified, as he reveals himself,
beneath the gale winds,
the cruel force of my predatory gaze.

There are seedlings in the snow, fragile green shoots,
that are tulips, that will be tulips,
as the sun assists them in their ascent.

I think of the way tulips look when they die;
the petals unfold and surrender their centre to the sun.

How the barren seeds cling faintly to the obdurate heart,
and perish, as they come undone.

Nancy Drew's Theatre of Blood

the truth loves me

— Sylvia Plath

The proprietor of Salome's is a
fallen man. Unloved, anxious,
but he smiles at me as I enter.
The pink walls are a Mardi Gras
of whips, chain mail and leatherette,
an apothecary of lotions, botanical
green condoms in red-petal foil.
The spiked dog collars, the manacles
seduce me: *Call in my death's-head
there; tie up my fears.*
But I want something playful,
a mask with oblong cat's eyes,
a tasselled merry widow.
I select Emotion Lotion and find it spreads like ice,
and then burns — like revenant fury —
under my tongue.
  My father leaves out details of
    her death, a *crossword cipher.*
    She was very unhappy;
      she often slept for hours in the afternoon.
    The rope, the noose is a ghost
      in the prisms of the chandelier,
    her footprints a fresco on the papered walls.
    The shattered jar on the parquet floor,
  laudanum, Vaseline, her blue negligee: an
apparition.

Because he is a lawyer, he defends her.
Pleasure eluded her;
she reached to the hot centre
of the sky, she tormented fate.

She knew the danger and rarely resisted.
He leaves me a pamphlet entitled *Autoerotic Hanging,*
he encourages me to leave her flowers,
prayers, by the toppled chair.
It is her cenotaph and it remains there.

But she remains close, she seems to
hold me in her arms and squeeze,
she is a sleek and dangerous python
who batters my senses. She sings, a burlesque
song of love. I detect a tremor in her voice,
You must be careful darling, there is a warp,
an imperfection

in the lens of my spyglass,
   that dangles over the field of black and white
   squares, the midriff of my dress.
   When the Queen has been sacrificed,
   the King is in danger.
     He moves slowly to the centre
     and the Bishop glides to meet him;
     she is radiant in a starched white apron,
     a three-cornered hat.
   She hands me heart-shaped cookies,
   fresh from the oven, and scrapes at Carson's
   shirtsleeves with salt and soda water
until the kiss, the feverish stain on
his neck and breastbone, disappears.

Hannah often vanishing as my mother's
plaintive voice called from the bedroom.
Quickly smoothing her hair, her sash,
and the rosewater of her flushed face.
She cried at the funeral, and I watched
tissue after tissue fall into her
crocodile purse.

Was his hand warm, urgent on her thigh,
is she still tender, still silent?

Their stolen moments, their ardour is X-rated,
erotic to me. Even as I reconstruct the murder,
their assignations excite my fancy
and I cherish them.
I am becoming more and more perverse.
 I want to join them someday,
   when the lights are low.
    Slipping into something more comfortable,
    the discipline number.
   You are your mother's daughter, he says,
  but the structure of S/M is fluid and changing,
 and it is the dominatrix who binds their faithless hands
together, exacting punishment.

I am all that remains of her;
detection also made her sick.
 But the urge to recover is less
compelling than the thrall,
 the passion of the truth that loves me.

Pearl

Nine Hammer Blows

for Kenneth Halliwell

John, we used the language as if we made it

— Robert Lowell

People don't like to be told
that you're sick
and then be forced
to watch
you
come
down
with the hammer.

— Anne Sexton

a deliberate form of frenzy — John, who sleeps so easily, and I,
setting out barbiturates, grapefruit juice: *If you read his diary all will*
be explained. Especially the latter part, I wrote,

and crushed his skull with nine hammer blows. He is still warm when
    I lie down.
My eyes closing, I see blood on the Magdalene, the mandolin, my design —

it has come to this. The latter part — eight pages — has disappeared,
    the diary ends
and what, what became of us in early August. It was painfully bright;
    I do not care
what others think, and pause at the black-spiked entrance gate,

drawing its points across my throat. You're sick, he says and leaves,
    more often these days, or
presses a napkin to the telephone. I hear murmured devotions, *soon, patience*
my love —

he loved me once, that I was sick, the things I saw. Spider monkeys in
roses, a ladder of cats' heads.

> *sometimes I love poverty,* a friend wrote; I miss everything.
> I was the first

to explain tragedy to him *(not wisely but too well),* to lubricate
    my fingers
and open him, tenderly easing the petals of the rosette, my tongue in his
    urethra, a taste of honey

much sweeter than wine, music, slipping between our single beds to kiss
    and the slow sedative
caress. The poppy is the first bloom I place on the walls, radiant, it
    pollinates the field

I attend with my paste and scissors. I do not have his facility with
    words, the orderly entries, dated,
detailed. The scent of cherry, urinal stones, the cup of a stranger's hand
    on his balls,

my orchids. I iron his briefs and pillowslips, trying to smooth the
    disorder, sheer terror is all I feel,
and the walls become heavy with paradise, marble gods recast, the
    choir invisible, angels striking

Moroccan princes. We were so still in the sand I thought we may
    never rise, the funereal
smoke of *kif* burning in censers, yellow-shirts embalming us with their
    religious lips.

I was his shadow, paling behind him a little cloud. The hammerclaws
    leave two impressions
on my palm. That he cannot leave me, so much is lost already (slivers
    of paper, haloes, shields),

how necessary shadows are. The fastened grey shape that retreats in
    pursuit, that may precede you.
Revealing your presence, gesturing to the distance of the sun,

I had to remove my clothing as I fell to my knees. Dying, you were still able
    to produce antiphony,
red flares of blood shining in the eclipse, the yellow fire in me.

Close to you I try to touch you, I see eight sheets fall like linens, like spirits.
As immaterial as purity, as sacred as the shadows

that seek me and falter, erased in the flames, a disclosure —

We went to bed early. Kenneth was looking wan.

Monday 31 July 1967.

I've Got You (Under My Skin)

just the thought of you makes me stop before I begin

Le Comte and I meet in discreet little corners to tender the tripled
      envelope and *chevaux-de-frise,*
skin-popping — unseen ormolu emblems, the lips of goddesses devised
      below the metal tines.

Perhaps it is hatred that lures me to these ravines or alleys, or the beguiling
feel of the long sleek rats making anklets of their tails. Casting shadows
in the blue night, he sails a fleet of gauze dressings

in the grey water that eavesdrops at our feet. And we visit restaurants
      in disguise;
my Cleopatra hair *comes undone* when he compares each violet
      tendril to ivy,
coronating the sun. Veils of ivy, the moon's black lashes

sweep its sweet yellow face, I am somewhere slow. Delicately he
      retrieves his pocket knife,
and in half circles of light stabs the spaces between my fingers.
I do not flinch, even as its reckless edges bite

accented initials, a monogram, in the folded linen napkins: *notre lune*
      de miel, my Count's
mouth is pursed, a scarlet stain, a memory of chokecherries, longing to taste

this poison, its red allure. Mars refracted, rubies pendent in gathers
      of Nile

silk is his look, lids lowered over jade-green eyes.

Folded like Japanese lanterns, *ancient oceans,* they draw me in.
      Easier to breathe beneath these
paper pagodas,

he dreams of mutilation:

>   O, *how sweet it is to snatch some child brutally*
> *from his bed*
> *to plunge your long nails into his soft breast*
> *and then you drink the blood.*

Because of its science and purity, sun-bleached fossils, the scorpion in
    resin, a matrix of colourless cells.

I look at the pale nimbus of his hair (the clouds that smother the sky)
    without apprehension.
My *ecstasy gone underground,* a cool white stone, and his ear, pressed
    to mine, is a pink shell,

Purplish Semele, I can almost hear the music. Whales moving in pods,
    their arias of love, the simplicity.
Of seawater on flesh, of motion, graceful, unconscious.

Bliss, that sinks under the points of spears; they colour the sea
    with their descent

and I count each fall, I watch his pallid face as we come down into despair,

familiar to us — we practise deception and we have obligations,
    promises to keep. Addiction is paramount,
the mainline, the *ethic of closeness,*

that is only consecrated when the needle enters,
and retrieves its taste of blood.

Have Gun, Will Travel
after Pam Grier

This is not vanity.
  Here error is all in the not done,
all in the diffidence that faltered.

— Ezra Pound

The mailbox at the foot of the stairs is tenantless; there is one Jesus
pamphlet — his arms outstretched, gesture. The depressions in his
    hands, bereft.

Moths circle the metal slot like gossamer, a skein of moths.

My own letters, vanished, unspeakable confessions: blackmail —
fields of iris — love retracting its yellow claws.

I have fewer friends. Tired of heartbreak, they avert their eyes,
    what have you done to yourself?
An incision, an accident: I have been impressed by his ardour,
    a memory of crescents, faint in the receding sky.

He loves me. I suffer his silence, its needles and pins, with pleasure.
    This is not vanity: the
Carmelite nuns that pass me on the street, their heads bowed, his arched collar,
    his vows, piety,

nausea. A terrible song — *It must be him, it must be him.* Reason occluded,
    a quarter sun in the dark field of spirits.
If stars assemble in language, clouds replicate the plush
    sphere of his mouth,

it must be him. I am dressed in my starched nurse-whites, the simple
    gown and three-cornered
hat, a red cross. As I place my cool blue lingerie, my hot-pink peignoir in a
    portmanteau,

this little gun of metal and pearl.

He confided in me that he was afraid of murder, poison, suffocation —
　　he wanted me to feel

dangerous. Secure that he may reserve his affection, the promises he
　　breaks: I will see you soon,
I meant to write, I think of you often.

How pleased he will be when I surprise him with the cool barrel,
　　when it arouses his neck, his temple.
Its sight lowers to the silver zipper, its cold teeth clenched,
　　closed to me

anxious for the hot kiss of lead, hollow points of fear and trembling.

I want to excite him this way. His loneliness lost as the razor emerges
　　from its sheath —
The long shining tail of the comet

that lights the sun in its orbit of ice.

There will he disarray, the inevitable blood I attend with bandages
　　and stitches; it flows
unstopped because my evening shoes are insensible, hard red alligator,

without comfort — in love there are certain contracts we are bound
　　to honour.

I will open his eyes with the edge of my leather gloves and there,
　　in the quiet white orbits, there is the moon,
that crept between us, still, in its membrane of shadows,

the promises the night remembers, and obeys.

Superfly

Make your mind what you want it to be.

— Curtis Mayfield

Tired of waiting for him, I think of a plan to stick it to the
Man — he waylaid me with promises: protection, his valuable keys.
Nights of seduction, I would glide to the curb in my customized Eldorado,
black finish and cool bubble top

and turn it over to a superyoung girl with rags and a bucket of soapy
water, with a smile and a dead president, *make it shine my sister.*
He is inside listening to Curtis, his sapphire ring —

he brings the moon with him, this cat, and his eyes glow like
mellow stones at my superfly threads. The cashmere white-stitched suit,
the maxi-coat trimmed in fox fur: *vixen,*

my pretty little hat with three blue feather plumes. I let him dig me
        for a while,
and lay a kiss, a spoon of cocaine on him, our secret meetings
a potent rush and I am hip to the hit to his fly hand on my thigh,

my ladies scatter in a cloud of Opium and he tells me,
you know me, I'm your friend.

I thought he was my man — I flash on him in the bathtub, its ledge of
        oils in flasks,
pulling a loofah sponge over my tired shoulders, passing a reefer
        in lemon paper,

on all the tired bitches working his keys, hustling his diamond rocks —
two sets of false eyelashes, micro-minis, freezing their asses off.

My .25 Beretta can't stop him, it's not real, I'm not real to him. He'll
use me up and kill me; I need brains guts and cool;
I put *fur* on your back, my baby, he says.

I am between him and death, *the greatest high of all,* and I ask him
    to step outside.
The pink flakes blow my mind and I turn to him with a flurry
    of karate kicks,
kicking out my left leg I bring him to the ground

and with my foot on the collar of his mohair suit I tell him, I took your
money and signed a contract on you: *I hired the best killers there are —*

men like you — *yeah, if one hair on my gorgeous head is harmed it's*
    all over for you.
It's all over for you, I think, as I imagine I am Superfly; my mind is
    what I want it to be,
the Man is tired and suddenly he looks

Old, very, very old as he turns away from me, the things he cannot dream —
my brazen plans, my *body full of love.*

Submission

for Mark and Debra: *Malleus Maleficarum*

The ground was never recovered, nor the legions, for their numbers were
thought so ill-omened that they never again appear in the army lists.

— J. M. Roberts

It begins with Diane — the gold shingles of her razored hair
alight in the wind that whips the trees,
the cotton slips pinned to nylon lines: these improbable ghosts.

The first I ever loved can still incite such desperation. Betrayal
lashes the careful stitches, the slight fabric;
its design undone.

She would take her switchblade and cut spiders in half —
a quadrant of scars radiating from her wrists and elbows, she wrote
        my name in blood,
let matches flare against the cuts,

small yellow head, searing. I used to operate on myself, she said.
Separate a triangle of skin and place objects — silver pins,
glass beads — close to the bone.

A private surgical kit, embroidery scissors, alcohol, fine needles,
and violet thread; silk, cat whiskers tied in complicated bows.
She remembers this way, where things are

where they are buried. We studied history together, this is how we
        met. Recovering the Roman
Empire; she draws military disasters in her margins, mail-clad
        horsemen pitching
violently to the ground, the movement of the cavalry

a swarm of locusts. Her silver compact slit open, because there are
        assassins in the narrow hallway;
her fine pale feet turn to form an arabesque (a delicate
        design of flowers,
leaves), furrows in the sheets and mattress,

pearls. Ropes of black pearls and a black rubber dress — submerged in
        the green haze,
the depths of a nightclub, listening. *Submission;* she hit his thighs
        with a chain, a hook in his mouth —

her lips were alluring. Red feather-quills, bright red flies. I think of
        him, brought violently
to the surface, his tensile body still below the thin edge of the filleting
        knife,
his slick flesh streaming as he surrenders — a ceremony of scales and
        gills, useless to him now,

as he breathes in and out. She told me once that she was like a
        scorpion, and I did not listen.
I let her creep between my fingers; danger was exotic to me then. I lived
        somewhere deep
beyond the coastline, in the crevices of rocks and wood-planks,

her gold hair spins like loose coins, strange and valuable. The
        currency of nightmares, where
the sun burns the earth and empties the seas — there are skeletons, gingerly
        reaching for night —

night will fall in a rustle of wings, the gentle sweep of the legs of
        scorpions.

Radiant Boys

for Stephen McDougall (1962–82)

*there are legends of Radiant Boys, the apparitions of a young boy
usually surrounded by a glowing light or flame.*

— Daniel Cohen

What was a cause for fear, doubt is now swept aside

— Horoscope, December 15, 1978

O the day I heard that, that he was dead — a panel truck at midnight,
    they identified
him by his teeth, arrowheads in the lattice-grille. He had been dead
    for years, to me.

My earliest ghost — the heat he emanated *(diving into the wreck);*
    I tormented him
with adoration, stealing his ephemera, a flannel square, his shaky
    signature razored from a textbook.

He was painfully shy, his head nestled in his collarbone, with defiant eyes:
he lived on the other side — visiting his family's house in secret, I tore
dead stalks of grass, ragweed, from the edges

where the lawn's decay kisses the street; I kiss

this strange bouquet, green fever spikes, my allergy to love. He would
    look at me, unsure,
his name written on my hands, my diffidence. Measuring the steps
    to his locker, his tree-fort,

he brought girls there with cherry wine, he called out their names
    — not mine.

And turning my own head away from him, terrified.

The soft skirt I bought, the colour of pumpkins. *Love's Baby Soft*
    blotted here
and there — embalm your wrist and throat in sweet pink, preserve
    this night.

There was a dance and I stood outside and saw him, apart from everyone,
dealing bags of grass. I watched the lights play *Stairway to Heaven* on
    his brass ring,
and he pulled me away to the bridge, *get higher baby,*

don't ever come down. He snaked his slender arms around me and
    scraped
his face against my hair, wanting to lick my lips, his hands lost in the
    supple orange,
the glow: *I try to talk to you and you won't look at me,*

I would not look at him then. Lost in his radiance and refusal,
    walking through fire,
luminous particles. The astrology that coursed beneath us: we turned
from the water, he turned to someone —

take care of her.

There is more and less: I came to meet him in an orchard and we bent
    together, bruised apples,
his tongue inquiring, what I could not offer.

Little stories — he washed his cat with Ivory soap, he left school early;
    he loved a girl.

Later, when I was far away, he told a friend: I know she is beautiful
    now, I can imagine this.

I found his death in an old newspaper — he had been trying to go
home. I never knew him, but speak to him still.

An apparition in a flame of light — he has things to tell me, that he
reached out, beyond the
circle of his own angry reticence, to surround me, the first time anyone
tried to minister the chills (how coldly I hated myself), to divine — that
I would live, imagining his beauty,

loving this radiant boy.

Condition

(of Louis Longhi: *the shampoo-killer*)

*Ladies and Gentlemen, we will not start with postulates but with an
investigation.*

— Freud, *Introductory Lectures on Psychoanalysis*

My condition begins in silence and stealth, prowling from salon to
      salon, stealing their
instruments. Clips and pins, wire rollers, foil sachets of shampoo and
      hot oil: *extreme unction.*

I lay with my arms crossed over my white smock, a garland of scissors
      and tongs.

In the institution I would lock myself away, excising strands of hair
      from soap cakes, from the
mouths of drains. Long red tendrils, white strands —

black cilia. Examining their roots under glass, the fertile bulbs, their
      fibrous shoots.
The tulips I planted with my father in plots of snow; his head was
      light in the winter sun,
untouchable.

They grew in rows, snail plairs — *shine, softness, and manageability;*
      I required this alone,
at first. That the hair must lie on its velvet pincushion like
      a diamond, that
certain strands must be placed

in the open doorway between my room and the dark corridor, where
      hairdressers pass in rubber gloves
and tinting aprons — their irons glowing hot, beguiling me

to the call. I never harmed them, the first girls — I arched their necks
        into bowls of steaming
water, and lathered their hair with lemon juice, sage soaked in cider vinegar,
        herbs I grew in window boxes,

my hands pulling clouds through these tresses. Replenishing
        the follicles and cells
from my germinal garden (the rosehip of their dresses).

The *hair ceremonial* that ended with Marie — I had set and combed
        her hair,
listened to its clean squeak when I stretched it into rats' tails and
        coronets. I was afraid and tied
her to a chair, gagged her, scared she may refuse.

To submit to further care — there are certain ways of doing things —
        I could not stand to think
of her tangling and distressing the locks, splitting the ends

of the slipknots. I washed her hair until there was no more shampoo,
        and then, in a delirium
I know is love, I continued with honey, detergent, witch hazel,
        bleach. As she struggled

she tightened the ropes, my grip tightened and she strangled to death.
I hid her in the earth *stricken with remorse* — the earth where
we set out the dull bulbs that would be tulips, switches of satin,
        yellow forelocks.

My father's head was covered with a golden down I longed to touch —
        when I reached out
with my child's fingers, he slapped them away.

I think of Marie, her uncovered skeleton, often. More often I trace
the forbidden contours of the crown.

In my dreams the baby tigers are gentle — they cling to me
as I stroke them, they tender me their warmth.

The Snake Pit
for Tony

I know the purity of pure despair

— Theodore Roethke

He is often tired this fall, his eyes — purple shadows,
narcotic flowers. Glassine bags, black envelopes, ill-concealed secrets
I discover, sunflower dust, faint streaks of powder.

His horror of water, its purity and the sweetness he desires;
his mouth is burnt sugar, a honeycomb
where gorgeous insects recline.

I am afraid of anger, exhaustion: I'm just tired, my mother would say,
    as she
retreated to her bed; she would not speak for days. James sleeps
    and wakes
in strange furies: *you've never loved me, you wish I could take you places —*

into the water, his body washing to the shore wreathed in seaweed
    and fire-coral.
Beyond recognition, he lies, and I believe him. Because I have my
    own secrets,

the same sweet tooth, the blue dissolution, a desire for serenity. When
the world is too much with me, and I revile myself,

forget to breathe. The first time I met him, shooting stars, once, twice,
my veins recoiled from the needle: *Is this what you want?*

I wanted to retreat, to see beautiful things — the scars on his wrists,
our dishevelled hair, the cracks in the tiles — transformed;

he once lived by the water, collecting dead flowers and fish bones. He
    came to me with nothing,
and never left. We began to assemble these things together.

Broken elemental objects, as mysterious in origin as he, as the
        painting he made,
where he levitates above me, dormant and formless,

I'm just tired, he said, and disappeared. Later, there is a call; he has
        been institutionalized,
a breakdown. I visit him often, finding him in the long antiseptic corridors,
in the ice of his prim white bed.

We listen to someone play the piano — *some say love, it is a river,*
        I kiss him,
and ask him to get better. At night, he combs the winter streets for
        heroin, and sinks deeper
into the glacial corners of his sheets.

When he finds his way through the bleak cold he sees something
        growing — a fast seedling,
unattended, irreducible. It is as trite and as ravishing as the tentative music
that played for us,

the seed, *that with the sun's love,* in the spring,

becomes the rose.

The Fly

Where we almost, nay more than married are.

— John Donne

Pearl egg of fly intimates the curve of larva, its spine and claw-point.
     The cellophane shell,
brittle pupa-blanket where the almost fly

lies like a spring. Coiled and tensile, its exertions will tear the sheet.
     Six black legs flutter
against the dry christening gown, I see his lambent eyes

cloistered in these living walls of jet.

Small glider, his veined wings are sheer parasols, gauzy skirts that
     admit the light. The orange
down of his pelvis beneath this architecture, blood is the adhesive

fastening flight, my sleek aviator presses his sucker feet to my lips.
     How little
he denies me, the drone in my ear and he swarms my heart if one

two light steps from the tips of my fingers he bows his head and
     makes a violin,

or hovers behind me when I circle the floor, lonely, he rests on
     shoulder, elbow, to
stare at me with swollen eyes,

darkling, drop of ink. A currant in the sugar dish, he models in the
     painted flowers, black eye
of Susan, blunt thorn — he delights in my decadence,

the slippery floor, tiles, and stairs haunted with illness: my sensual life
  and his intersect.
He comes on the wing of another spring, in slicks of grey water, the
  pendant sun.

To navigate what is unknown to me, patiently, he regards the chrysalis of
  skin that envelops

the arched veins. Incurious and constant, he is used to waiting for the
  modest blush, the rustle of disrobing

the hush. Of silks unfolding, of gossamer veils drawn as tenderly as
  breath, from the fluent sea
of *one blood made of two,* the sweetness of his pestilent kiss.

Ambrosia

To thrust all that life under your tongue!

— Anne Sexton

There is always the smell of chocolate, the rich dark swirl
and I separate his wildflower curls when he sleeps:
      Stephen only stayed for moments. Moonlight spooned into our bed,
his red cross grazed my lips, I tasted cherries, his

innocent hand in the night road, calling me — *o la paloma blanca,*
      the radio played this
and he smiled, his mouth

the cranberries we stir into the copper vessels, their skin splits and
      offers bitter fruit.

He became restless: *the guy wanted to leave and I didn't want him to leave.*

A heart-shaped box, the candies are moss green; I have held on to this
      too long. Anger hot
enough to incinerate each scalloped chocolate I fold into gold foil and twist

his head around, it breaks, I crush his throat with a metal paddle (stolen
from the factory, sweetness is only mine to steal),

wrap his confectionary body into plastic bags, and then retrieve it.

To kiss the rigid wrists and neck that belong to me, sledgehammer
smashes each bone into crystals, stars entombed in stalks of grass.

My first love affair still glitters, when I am here

scattering starlets of cleaning powder on the tile floor, my orange
      coveralls, the moon that
tempered him,

by the trees and streetlights, his semaphore fingers spelling Jeffrey, Jeffrey,
for he creeps,

when the first blow reaches my face, I have already retreated. Into
    romance, the rapture.
I held them close

all that life under my tongue, unyielding in my arms, their hollow
    eyes like truffles in cream,
looking back at me.

As a child, I would preserve insects in formaldehyde, dragonflies,
    spiders, a praying mantis.
I fall to my knees in a glaze of pain and remember entreating them,
    don't leave me,
don't leave me please, and what I read,

what I read today: *In those days shall men seek death and shall not
    find it.* My eyes close
like gilded paper, and I find it and

death, my love, does not leave.

After Illness

February returns — a ribbon of pink, a paper wand sealed in ice. Blue
star, a girl in violet tulle and diamante glitter brocades her little bodice.

Pain, my familiar, retreats like the bursts of light that radiate the sky,
    at times
a galaxy of signifiers arises. Erasing what is liminal, the white lip of snow,

sheer slips of opal, enveloping the earth below.

He moves between these lines — *the individual* — in a crown of fire.
    Religion as sacrifice, to hold
the white bird, bind its wings in wire,

and slit its throat. I would draw him closer in a ritual of purity, what I
    did not know.

He came to me in violence and romance. How this winter ceremony
    descends — gangsters
fall in midnight's alley; children in altar gowns, their necks are slight
    white feathers,

each tendon sliced as blood lilts — *Ave Maria,* songs of love. A serenade

in an empty room. The Vietnamese proprietor assembling mirrored
    lights and monitors,
he sang, *I was dreaming of the past.* His hair white with sleeplessness,
    numinous dreams.

His vertebrae abrading, spineless, he reveals his horror of himself —

    at whose sight all the stars Hide their diminished heads.

The infernal serpent's voice of sulphur and liquid pearl rises beneath
      the red lights where
we have coiled like snakes alight with diamonds. I slither toward the
      hands that will scratch in
trident scars,

the small of my back, at once, asleep. I have been desperately tired,
and he irons this sickness from me in smooth circles.

On a bed of flowers, a pattern of vines and berries. Trace the angry
      letters raised on his flesh,
the ashen clouds, his beauty corrupted, still luminous

as angels are. I must reveal my own dreams in time.

Betrayal, a glacial half-slip, the chill of her fingers breaking into
      blossom, the ice an apparition
the blade divides.

The blue line that creates spheres, defense. His face mutable, implores
      me to assist him.
Afraid of grief, he offers his heart. Creased and ephemeral, it begins
      to discolour the snow

where I have passed, at last, the spirits uncovered. Meaningless stars
without radiance, a metonym, faithless —

the pallor that comes after illness, after its first feverish blush.

Fetish

I'm really sick when it comes to socks . . . They're parts of the
combination to the deepest, most secret recesses of my mind.

— Ted Bundy

It's one of my fantasies —

        a wooden pharmaceutical chest, drawer after drawer, filled
    with socks. In crisp cellophane envelopes, the colours of the sky

at sunset when I sheathe my *attractive feet* in ribs of black with
    yellow bands
and gather my sticks and gloves, the false sling

starched and clean, secured to my shoulder. Later there is a sense of
    sorrow, remorse,
etcetera; I dislike the other field. Dried leaves and disorderly
    scratches, from
branches, her urgent fingernails

the pain in my hands. I soak them in a basin of warm water and admire
    each clever finger
following the even rows, the letters of the law in my own defense.

I object, the girls all looked the same — that girl with money enough to
    fill each drawer
with a ransom of wool and cotton — spinning gold from a wheel,

spinning when I see the part in her dark hair; her eyes are avarice,
    deflecting me.

I would wear my one pair of socks and underwear and rinse them
    in the sink, the sight of them —
deriding me from the shower rod, threadbare

hooked like signs: the police in Pensacola found traces of her hair,
Even there I was buying socks everywhere.

I am too fine for this, I want to lay out my affluence in sleek pairs,

have her lie among the elastic and silk, like a daisy: *It makes me sad
            because I've never seen*
such — such beautiful socks before.

I imagine it is someone else, tearing their bodies apart, their skin
            in his teeth,

the bite mark that is my undoing, the distinctive curve of poverty: I said
that they were pinned up every night,

I did not mention they were red — they left pale blood-pools on the
            enamel, the white
expanse of their ruined thighs;

*I always felt that I would have really made it if I had all the socks and
underwear I could ever use,*

if I could tear this from one girl or another, her fault.

And somehow find the ecstasy (her last breath pulled slowly from her
            throat), hidden
in the secret recesses,

the deepest pangs —

I had to restructure my life, from the beginning, I was always so cold.
It may have affected me, alight with fever, I slip her over me.

She is argent, the sheen of the fleshings
            folded together, lip to toe like rose petals in my bed,
my bed of roses.

Amaryllis

Let go,
please, your heart is not that strong
— Neil Eustache

You can't miss me, he said. And I waited for him at the long wooden
    table, absorbed
in a cooking show; venison wrapped in cabbage leaves,

the green armature. I have learned to protect myself from strangers; I
    write messages on cocktail
napkins, *leave me alone, leave me.*

He walks toward me, his face dispassionate, one tooth absent, a cryptic
    space like superstition.
The region between ladders, where spirits gather. And evanesce above
    crossed fingers,

souls retreating from faith.

The *beauty that does not die* at the centre of his terrible stories. The
    stranger who caressed him
as he slept, who lost his car keys and desire — William retrieves himself

in memory and ceremony. Smoothing the earth of his mother's grave,
    his basement room, where
he lay, coronated in candles, his mother's voice.

The violence that marks his hands, a broken finger, unspeakable
    fights — *be a man,* he brands
this on his back with hot wire. With irony, because he is tender, without.

He draws a map for me of Kamloops, a sepulchre with a circle, an
    arrow: where I come from,
where I have been. Bereft, without belief, he offers me charity. Reaches to
    me and lifts my
abject face;

we will meet in accident. To plan a mink farm, there are minks loose
        everywhere, what we
refuse to kill;

at the *Lanterne Verde,* in an unravelled sweater, a shadow of grey and
        lichen green,

to see the gardens that are cased in glass.

The day he left, we looked at one-eyed fish in the leaden stream. The
        air was sleepy, as sultry
as the silk-red amaryllis

that bent their narrow blooms in sorrow.

He left me with this, and something else — perennial, his counsel. Your
        bones are
made this way. Emerald stalks, between flower, resisting loss, secure
        and certain

in the shelter, of the green house.

all my seasick sailors

Sly and second-sighted, my friends have abandoned ship. Rats,
    escaping in small grey
lifeboats, their annular tails turn the tide, their lambent eyes, like the
    moon, dictate its flow.
The violinist plays "Autumn" as the masts unfold, water lilies in the
    pitch of the sea.

A message in semaphore, what I have always longed to know — to stand
    by the stern, and
with courage, let go. Nostalgia's poison

love spreads out like a sheaf of photographs, memory without blood,
    a fluked anchor,
undone. The line that breaks when the storm comes, the truth that
    sailors know:
red skies without delight,

a bad sign. To navigate you must know where you are going, with an
    exact chart,
pin-stuck with ellipses. Accidents, typhoon, the fibrous stakes of sea
    monsters, the diamond ice caps,

miracles that have changed course, carved passages into the new
    worlds, where sailors
arise. In white militia,

letters come like gulls flat on the crest of waves, infatuation coursing,
    like a science of chaos,

they appear in envelopes of ice, intermittent ghosts — to remind me
    that love is spectral,
unforeseen.

The rapids were turbulent toward the Asian corridor, sailing into
        Lachine. It is China, after all.
Rare and fragile, esteemed from a great distance,

protected in shelf-ice.

I touch this china from rim to stem, and feel its raised flowers,
        brought to me from the ocean's
floor. *In spite of the danger,* the mariners have garlanded the stingray
— as the lashings narrowed,

they retrieved me from the wreck.

Geography
for Daniel Jones

i. Love

To see him I would walk to Grace, past the windows of hooks — calves
     with their brown-paper
gowns, lobsters sinking in kale-green tanks. Their premonitory eyes
     are flat dead stones.

Ephemera designed to obscure memory, glass jars of seeds, vines of
     purple grapes.
He spoke to me with difficulty; admissions I cannot remember, but
     his hands,
his lips are still

stained with violet. I meant to say I loved him; I did not.

I came to Grace, measuring his loathing for things esoteric to him —
irregular grammar, wild dogs, all vegetables — some terrible dream of
     red cabbage,
its radiant veins and leaves

           suffocating him, that his bones and blood would flourish,
that he may live, that he may

continue to suffer my own sadness with a silence particular to him.
     A silence I did not know was
fraught with anger, night terrors: a cerement of spider filaments,
     their slender malice.

The small parameters he drew for safety. We walked within these lines
without deviation, encompassed by stars, he could almost breathe, he
     could chart
the fever of hatred that spikes as it turns inward

unsettling him. I have seen the artifacts and ruins,
his derelict bathtub — there was a drama there, his first death.

It is arduous, approaching grace. You must continue, trace the narrow
      lines of its map, and be
prepared. To draw the blade neatly,

divide your wrists into continents. Rivers are created, tributaries,
      fault lines —
geography's red and blue relief, where forgiveness lies remote
and uncharted.

ii. Anger

Anger comes between us — the street's topography, black branches
      stitch its grey
surface, an arbitrary parallel. I am superstitious when I pass his window,
the blue light where he works, a faint plume of smoke in the
      darkened panes.

Anger that is fatal if it is unspoken, anaesthesia without surgery,
      cyanide tables in mid-
fall: the brittle leaves break as I gather them, seedpods spin —

pollen wraiths, wasp-fossils in glass — the time he removed its bite
      with iodine and I
cried, his hands extracting venom and now
erasing me, plotting my demise. The tragedian that he is, that I am

performing the final act *(The weight of this sad time we must obey)* in
      Kensington Market.
Where palm trees and impatiens were, there are skeletal cats,
crates of decadent vegetables, there is John

repelling me and I write, later: *how did I not see his hatred,* the sable leaves
of artichokes unfolding, poison at the centre.

I withdraw from the sting, *peripeteia* — his sudden ruin a tiresome
      convention.
He was capable of cruelty; he was meticulous, theatrical. His shaven
      head a courtesy,
facilitating the coroner's scalpel

the measure of the radius (once an aurora of pain), faint tremors,
the uneasy crown of fury, relinquished. I pass by him, several times,
    my head bowed
in fear and contempt.

Until the day 1 looked again, where I imagined he was, his door closed
    that he would open to
me, what he had offered me. Light, clarifying the pearl, the cautious
    fracture that
injures the membrane. He set out cups and saucers, expecting me;
    I ascended

the perilous steps toward him. *I miss you,* I thought, as the sun
    streaked like an urchin, and
punished his delicate heart.

iii. Loss

He came home on a Friday, sick, and stayed in the back room with
      bowls of soup
and napkins. A crumpled blanket, a small writing pad. *Frog Moon*
      underlined,
the door locked, bad news

collected elsewhere. Things are shrinking, this one room —
the snow drifts, a border of chrysanthemum, encompassing
the enclosure, the necropolis: *Il Gatto Nero,* the Golden Wheat —

where we met and you spilled your coffee — happy to see me, sweet
friend I had forgotten

your rare, infectious bliss.

Lost, you left signs I read backwards: *a day in early winter without plan,*
without direction, incomprehensible and monstrous,

you left nothing, stacks of empty boxes, no ventilation in the plastic bag
that smothers the death rattle. You left

and were carried down the stairs, in the indifferent hands of the ushers,
rubber gloves closing your eyes, yellow police-tape pushed
through the bannisters,

carnival. One Easter we watched this from your window, the stations
      of the cross,
the figure of Veronica, her ghost-veil pressed to her white robe, passing

as religious, I solemnly unpeel the 2. from your door, it leaves a
      little space.
There are emerald draperies in your windows now, I see the lush
      leaves
of monsteria plants.

The new number that is fastened there. It is slight, a slip of paper that
    will be torn away
when the winds begin again, when the ice and early darkness come.
    To fall in reverence,
what you alone discovered —

Grace.

Acknowledgements

I wish to thank Martha Sharpe, my editor Kevin Connolly, and Michael Holmes, my *ambrosia*, for their valuable assistance and support. Also, many thanks to Mary Crosbie, Bruce McDonald, Adrienne Leahey, Rick, and Chris Russo, wherever you are.

Quote on page 64 from "Howard Hears Marion Downstairs," from *Lardcake* (Toronto, ECW Press, 1996) by David McGimpsey.

Excerpts from "Live," on page 123, and "Wanting to Die," on page 36, from *Live or Die* by Anne Sexton. Copyright © 1966 by Anne Sexton, reprinted by permission of Houghton Mifflin Co. All rights reserved.

Excerpt on page 123 from *Notebook* by Robert Lowell. Copyright © 1970 by Robert Lowell. Reprinted by permission of Farrar, Straus & Giroux, Inc.

Quote on page 123 from Jeffrey Conway's correspondence used by permission of the author.

Quote on page 128 from "Canto LXXXI" by Ezra Pound. Copyright © 1966, 1968 by Ezra Pound. Used by permission of New Directions Publishing Corporation.

Quote on page 132 from *History of the World* by J. M. Roberts. Used by permission of the author and the Peters Fraser & Dunlop Group.

Quote on page 140 from Theodore Roethke, "In a Dark Time," *The Collected Poems of Theodore Roethke* (Bantam Doubleday Dell Publishing Group, Inc.). Used by permission.

Quotes on pages 148-49 from *Ted Bundy: Conversations With a Killer by* Stephan G. Michaud & Hugh Aynesworth. Copyright © 1989 by Stephan L Michaud and Hugh Aynesworth. Used by permission of Dutton Signet, a division of Penguin Books USA Inc.

Quote on page 150 from Neil Eustache, *You Can't Take Any More,* an unpublished manuscript, by permission of the author.

Quote on page 158 from Alain Robbe-Grillet, *The Erasers* (Translation by Richard Howard; Grove/Atlantic, Inc.:1964). Used by permission.

Note from the publisher: Every reasonable effort has been made to contact the holders of copyright for materials quoted in this work. The publishers will gladly receive information that will enable them to rectify any inadvertent errors or omissions in subsequent editions.)

LYNN CROSBIE WAS born in Montreal and is a cultural critic, author, and poet. A Ph.D. in English literature with a background in visual studies, she teaches at the University of Toronto and the Art Gallery of Ontario. Her books (of poetry and prose) include *Pearl, Liar,* and *Life Is About Losing Everything.* She is also the author of the controversial book, *Paul's Case* and the editor of *The Girl Wants To.* She is a contributing editor at *Fashion,* and a National Magazine Award Winner who has written about sports, style, art, and music.

A LIST

The A List

The Outlander · Gil Adamson

The Circle Game · Margaret Atwood

Survival · Margaret Atwood

The Hockey Sweater and Other Stories · Roch Carrier

Roch Carrier's La Guerre Trilogy · Roch Carrier

Queen Rat · Lynn Crosbie

The Honeyman Festival · Marian Engel

Eleven Canadian Novelists Interviewed by Graeme Gibson · Graeme Gibson

Five Legs · Graeme Gibson

De Niro's Game · Rawi Hage

Kamouraska · Anne Hébert

Ticknor · Sheila Heti

No Pain Like This Body · Harold Sonny Ladoo

Civil Elegies · Dennis Lee

Ana Historic · Daphne Marlatt

Like This · Leo McKay Jr.

The Selected Short Fiction of Lisa Moore · Lisa Moore

Alden Nowlan Selected Poems · Alden Nowlan

Poems For All the Annettes · Al Purdy

This All Happened · Michael Winter